Contents

Executive Summary

![São Paulo cityscape with Faria Lima Avenue]

Faria Lima Avenue in São Paulo, Brazil, has been redeveloped with funds obtained from additional building rights auctioned in the stock market through special bonds (CEPACs).

Urbanization in Latin America is associated with strong pressure for the supply of serviced land, resulting in significant changes in land values that are distributed unequally among landowners and other stakeholders. Conventional fiscal policies and instruments largely neglect how the costs of providing urban infrastructure and services are socialized, and how their benefits are privatized.

The notion of value capture is to mobilize for the benefit of the community at large some or all of the land value increments (unearned income or *plusvalías*) generated by actions other than the landowner's, such as public investments in infrastructure or administrative changes in land use norms and regulations. The region has a long history with value capture policies, and many countries, notably Brazil and Colombia, have passed explicit legislation calling for consideration of value capture principles. Nevertheless, national legislation has been found to be neither necessary nor sufficient to allow some jurisdictions to use this potentially powerful financing mechanism to implement a variety of tools adapted to their local needs.

This discussion of the concept of value capture explains its justification and increasing popularity, provides a brief review of its antecedents in Latin America and elsewhere around the world, and illustrates its many forms and longstanding presence in the urban planning agenda. The reasons for its growing popularity are manifold: regional economic stabilization and fiscal decentralization; more progressive strategies for urban planning and management; re-democratization, increased social awareness, and demands for equitable public policy responses; changing attitudes toward privatization and public-private partnerships; the influence of multilateral agencies; and pragmatic considerations to capture land value increments to raise funds for local community needs.

The report examines three categories of voluntary and compulsory applications of tools affecting existing, new, or changing land uses in single or multiple property development projects: property taxation and betterment contributions; exactions and other direct negotiations for charges for building rights or for the transfer of development rights; and large-scale approaches such as development of public land through privatization or acquisition, land readjustment, and public auctions of bonds for purchasing building rights.

Performance indicators of revenues, other private investments generated by value capture, and the effects of higher transaction transparency and corruption mitigation in the land market vary significantly among comparable jurisdictions applying the same tool. Although in most places revenues are still low, the applications of betterment contributions in Bogotá and CEPACs in São Paulo have generated revenues in excess of a billion dollars for those cities. At the same time, the broader dissemination of these and other instruments is often blocked by powerful stakeholders (notably landowners) and by opinion leaders (including academics) from both sides of the ideological spectrum due to a lack of understanding of the theoretical rationale and basic operational issues involved in the implementation of value capture policies and tools.

Accordingly, this review of value capture in Latin America recommends steps that can be taken in three spheres: learning from varied experiences with the implementation of value capture policies and tools; increasing knowledge about the complex nature of varied value capture approaches; and promoting greater understanding among public officials and citizens about how value capture tools can be used to benefit their communities.

Learn from Implementation Experiences: While value capture charges in theory are neutral regarding land use and should fall entirely on landowners, in practice successful implementation demands management skills to deal with many complex factors and diverse stakeholders. In addition it requires proper understanding of land market conditions, comprehensive property monitoring systems, a fluid dialogue among fiscal, planning, and judicial entities, and the political resolve of local government leaders.

Increase Knowledge about Theory and Practice: Conducting research, documenting and disseminating implementation experiences, and providing evidence about how value capture policies work on the ground are essential to overcome the disjunction between rhetoric and practice and to change the behavior and attitudes of public officials, landowners, and the community at large.

Promote Greater Public Understanding and Participation: Land value increments are captured more successfully from landowners and other stakeholders who perceive they are receiving greater benefits from a public intervention than those accruing from business as usual. Furthermore, value capture tools are more likely to succeed when used to solve a locally recognized problem.

CHAPTER 1

Latin American Urbanization and the Case for Value Capture

© ALVARO URIBE

High-density development in the Barra da Tijuca area of Rio de Janeiro was built in the 1970s and 1980s as envisioned in the master plan of 1969.

Urbanization in Latin American has produced a formidable set of urban problems ranging from vast, often illegally occupied areas with minimal urban services to rampant disregard for building and land use regulations in wealthier neighborhoods in some cities. This state of affairs cannot be attributed exclusively to broader macroeconomic factors that contribute to urban poverty, but also to how the provision of urban infrastructure and services is financed, how land uses are managed, and how property rights are determined.

Rapid urbanization over the last century led to the emergence of a vigorous land market, and windfalls resulting largely from public interventions reinforced strong land-owning interests. When fiscal and human resources are relatively scarce, the provision of urban infrastructure and services in those areas that can support higher densities creates significant increases in land value. These linkages between services and prices allow ample room for practices such as active land speculation (Jaramillo 1994), clientelism, and other kinds of influence (including corruption) between public and private interests. This is why land ownership is such an important issue in the urban land policy agenda, and why the spatial allocation of public investment is so vulnerable to abuse and favoritism by well-positioned stakeholders (Smolka 2011).

UNEARNED INCOME FROM PUBLICLY PROMOTED URBANIZATION

The expectation that land may be designated for future urban uses or redevelopment can produce significant land price hikes, even before any public investments actually begin. The opening of the Barra da Tijuca neighborhood of Rio de Janeiro in the 1970s illustrates the impact of selective investment on land value increments (box 1.1).

Over and above the unearned income accrued to a privileged few, which could otherwise be used to fund public investments, unaccounted-for social costs often result from biased public decision making. The political economy of Latin American urbanization offers many examples of questionable (inefficient, unequal, unsustainable) public decisions regarding the spatial allocation of investments in urban infrastructure and services and the use of arbitrary land use norms and regulations. It is not hard to see how the prospect of accruing windfalls from such public interventions may induce complicity between landowners and regulators.

For example, no plans have been implemented around the petrochemical complex in Itaboraí, near Rio de Janeiro, to capture part of the enormous increment in land value generated by extensive public investment that could help finance much-needed urban infrastructure (box 1.2). Moreover, an effective urban planning and financing policy has not yet been proposed to prevent the growth of informal settlements amidst a booming real estate market fueled by high concentrations of public and private investment (Salandia 2012).

MULTIPLIER EFFECTS OF LAND USE CHANGES

The stakes are high when it comes to the land value increments resulting from public

BOX 1.1
Barra da Tijuca, Rio de Janeiro

The Barra da Tijuca area, covering 82 square kilometers (km²) of developable land, provided an opportunity for extension of the city's high-income South Zone. It constituted 10 percent of the city of Rio de Janeiro, and half of Baixada de Jacarepagua, an area of 160 km² including a 20 km beachfront and 122.50 km² of developable land.

Expensive public transit lines were announced in 1967 to open this area for expansion in response to pressure from developers for more attractive, buildable areas. In 1969 the city hired Lucio Costa, the urban planner responsible for Brasilia's master plan in the 1950s, and his proposal for this neighborhood was approved in the same year. Direct access through tunnels and an elevated expressway built in 1974, together with the master plan, were associated with an increase in land value of 1,900 percent from 1972 to 1975. In the same period, land prices in most other high-valued areas of Rio appreciated about 435 percent (Vetter, Massena, and Rodrígues 1979).

The plan's land uses and building standards were implemented in 1976 (Rezende 1982; 2005). The process was accompanied by frenetic land acquisitions leading to the control of almost 30 percent of the new developable area by only three landowners. By 1980 one developer had accumulated more than 6 km² of land, or about 8 percent of the whole area. Some of these acquisitions are still under legal investigation.

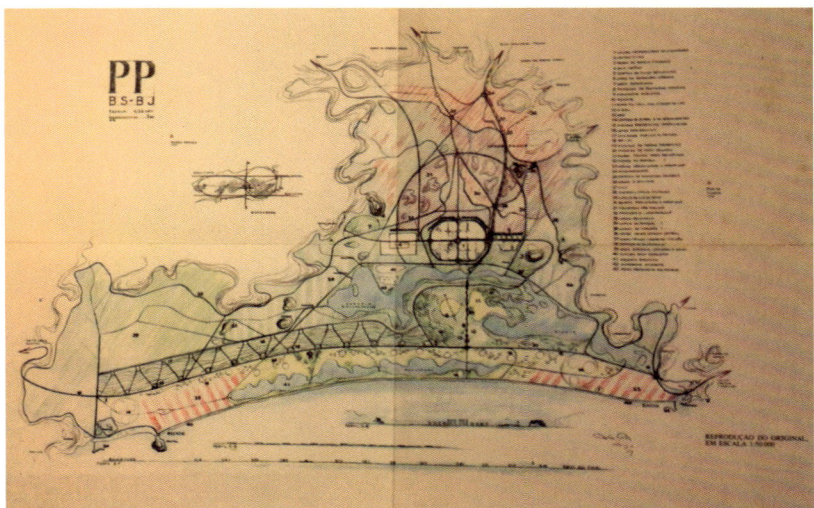

Proposed Master Plan of Barra da Tijuca by Lucio Costa, 1969

SOURCE: ORIGINAL PLAN FROM THE MUNICIPAL ARCHIVE OF RIO DE JANEIRO

intervention, whether in large complex developments such as Itaboraí or in smaller areas. The so-called urban multiplier—the ratio of the per square meter price of land

BOX 1.2
Itaboraí Petrochemical Complex, Rio de Janeiro

As a consequence of the discovery and exploitation of the pre-salt layer of oil reserves off the coast of Rio de Janeiro, in 2006 Brazilian Petrobras announced the construction of a petrochemical complex on the east side of the metropolitan region in the municipality of Itaboraí (population of 218,000 in 2010). Work started in 2008, and in 2009 Petrobras announced the expansion of the original project doubling the capacity of the refinery that is to become operational in 2015. The Petrochemical Complex Rio project (COMPERJ) occupies an area of 5,400 hectares, and investments of over US$21 billion are expected to generate up to 150,000 jobs (Petrobras 2013).

The complex, located near the end of Rio's new beltway, the Arco Metropolitano, has so far stimulated 160 new businesses; commercial and office spaces are now sold at US$7,000/m² for a property gain of 40 percent in 2009 alone. A plot of unserviced land in a subdivision that previously sold for about US$14/m² has quadrupled in price to US$55/m². At the same time, slums are now rampant in this otherwise high-end real estate market where, according to the Regional Council of Realtors of the State of Rio de Janeiro, properties have appreciated over 70 percent from 2009 to 2012. There is little evidence, however, that Itaboraí is developing a financial strategy to capture this increased value and implement plans for a pleasant, sustainable, and socially equitable urban environment.

TABLE 1.1
Effects of Administrative Land Use Changes on Land Prices (Stylized Facts)

Type of Land Use Change	Price before Change (US$/m²)	Increment (%)	Price after Change (US$/m²)	Windfall on 5,000 m² (US$)
Rural to Urban Conversion	2	400	10	40,000
Building Norms	100	80	180	400,000
Zoning Regulations	200	100	400	1,000,000

Source: Prepared by the author.

designated for urban uses to its pre-existing rural (agricultural) use value at the urban fringe—is typically over 4:1.

In Quito, Ecuador, the urban multiplier was estimated at five times the value of non-urbanized land in the Amagasi Inca neighborhood (Barcia and Ortiz 1996). Comparing average or median values per square meter of property transactions over 10,000 m² with those of plots from 250 to 600 m² for zones in the urban fringe of Rio de Janeiro, a statistically robust multiplier of six was found over the period from 1968 to 1984 (Smolka 1994). More recently, Vetter, Massena, and Vetter (2011) used survey data for Rio's West Zone to find a 4.29 multiplier. Data collected globally by Angel and Mayo (1996) ratifies this order of magnitude for land value increments.

The local provision of investments in urban infrastructure and services elicits three types of land use change (land use conversion; higher densities, footprints, or other building norms; and zoning regulations) that constitute important sources of windfalls for well-placed landowners. Allowing for higher densities (floor area ratios or FARs) or changing zoning from residential to commercial uses generates handsome increments, albeit usually lower (in relative terms) compared to rural to urban land use conversions where the base value is low (table 1.1). Reliable data on the effects of changing norms on land prices are difficult to obtain, and few studies are available.

Bank transactions on changes in land use from residential to commercial in Colonia San Benito in San Salvador, El Salvador, reviewed by real estate assessor Gustavo Sagastume, suggested a land value appreciation of 108 percent, from US$196 to US$407/m² in 2004. Similarly, information drawn from a developers' data bank on property transactions in Bogotá suggested changes ranging from 59 to 151 percent, depending on the neighborhood (Borrero Ochoa 2007). The same source shows land value changes ranging from 80 to 100 percent when converting single-story homes into residential buildings of five or six stories, and additional increments of 40 percent for eight-to-twelve-story buildings.

WINDFALLS FROM INVESTMENTS IN URBAN INFRASTRUCTURE

A comprehensive study conducted in three major cities of Brazil (Brasilia, Curitiba, and Recife) revealed significant differences in land value increments for plots at different locations and distances from the urban center, according to the types of services provided (Serra, Dowall, and da Motta 2005). For example, the increased value per square meter of an inner ring plot from supplying water, pavement, or sewerage is much higher than that of plots in the outer ring. The differences vary with the combination of services available (table 1.2). In all cells, except for the provision of sewerage in the middle and outer rings, the land value increment exceeds the cost of providing the service. The exceptions are because the lower density in the outer rings allows individuals to install alternative sewerage facilities more easily than to access water supplies or build roads.

The investment cost to provide services is much lower than the resulting land value increment, supporting Donald Shoup's (1994, 236) poignant question: "Why is it so difficult to fund public infrastructure that increases the value of serviced land by more than the cost of the infrastructure itself?" Given Latin America's chronically insufficient supply of serviced land, high levels of urban poverty, and the lag between the tax base and social needs, the land value increment could provide a substantial source of funding to mitigate these chronic problems, rather than provide substantial windfalls to private landowners.

For example, in areas predominantly occupied by the urban poor, such as the West Zone of Rio de Janeiro, fully serviced land was priced at US$145/m^2 in 2011 compared to formal undeveloped land sold at US$34/m^2 (Vetter, Massena, and Vetter 2011). Similar values have been found in the Global Urban Indicators database for 13 cities with over 500,000 inhabitants in different countries (UN-Habitat 2008).

However, the cost of fully servicing land intended for low-cost housing developments in compliance with urban codes ranges from US$10 to US$35/m^2, depending on topographical conditions, quality of the infrastructure, and scale of the project. These prices and costs demonstrate the potential for the use of land value increments to fund public investments even in the lower end of the land market (Bouillon 2012).

TABLE 1.2
Land Price Increments (US$/m^2) Related to Plot Location in Brazilian Municipalities, 2001

Increment for Additional Services	Distance to Central Business District			Investment Cost of Service Provision for 1000 m^2 of Usable Area
	5–10 km (inner ring)	15–20 km (middle ring)	25–30 km (outer ring)	
+ Water	11.10	5.10	3.20	1.02
+ Pavement	9.10	4.80	3.40	2.58
+ Sewerage	8.50	1.80	0.30	3.03

Source: Adapted from Serra, Dowall, and da Motta (2005).

THE PRINCIPLES OF VALUE CAPTURE

Value capture refers to the recovery by the public of the land value increments (unearned income or *plusvalías*) generated by actions other than the landowner's direct investments (figure 1.1). Although all such increments are essentially unearned income, value capture policies focus primarily on the increment generated by public investments and administrative actions, such as granting permissions for the development of specific land uses and densities. The objective is to draw on publicly generated land value increments to enable local administrations to improve the performance of land use management and to fund urban infrastructure and service provision.

The notion is that benefits provided by governments to private landowners should be shared fairly among all residents. Furthermore, the principle that no citizen should accumulate wealth that does not result from his own efforts, known as "unjustified enrichment with no cause" (*enriquecimiento sin justa causa*), is prevalent in most Latin American constitutions (Rabello de Castro 2012).

A typical value capture application would have the government recover only that portion of land value increases created by its direct interventions. A broader application would have the government recover any land value increase from actions other than those of the landowner—for example, those resulting from the direct impact of market forces associated with a general increase in

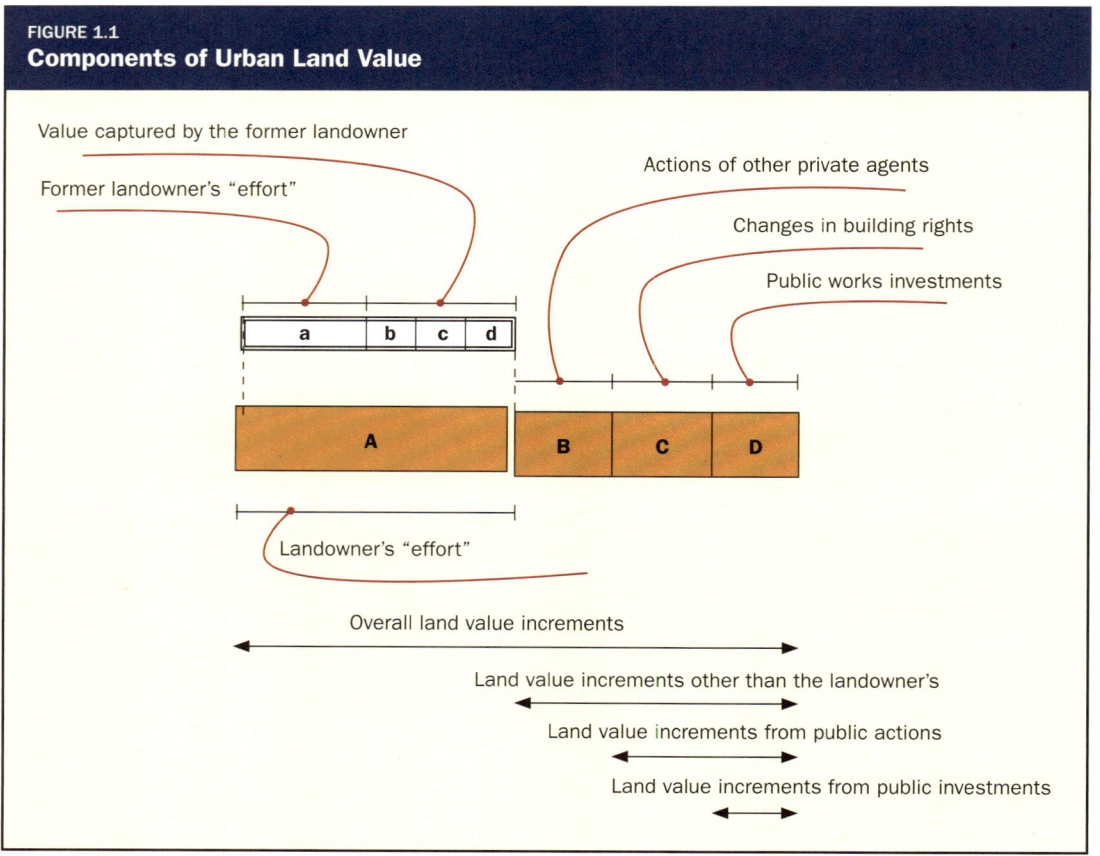

FIGURE 1.1
Components of Urban Land Value

Value captured by the former landowner

Former landowner's "effort"

Actions of other private agents

Changes in building rights

Public works investments

a   b   c   d

A   B   C   D

Landowner's "effort"

Overall land value increments

Land value increments other than the landowner's

Land value increments from public actions

Land value increments from public investments

Source: Adapted from Furtado, Biassotto, and Maleronka (2012).

urban population or from the indirect impacts on land values from the use of subsidies for housing and urbanization services. In Chile such subsidies resulted in land values increasing 316 percent from 1994 to 2004, ultimately absorbing 84 percent of the increase from the government's adjustments in the vouchers to keep up with rising housing prices (Brain and Sabatini 2006).

Other more geographically limited examples may relate to the legitimacy of windfalls resulting from proximity to newly discovered archeological sites or from dramatic changes in a neighborhood, such as new "celebrity" residents or retailers, that make it more fashionable and thus more valuable for others in the area. In all these cases the property owners did nothing directly to enhance their land values. Thus, all or part of the increased value should be shared with the public (Brown and Smolka 1997).

This report focuses on land value changes resulting from direct government actions or community efforts. Accordingly, value capture is the process by which some of the land value increments attributed to government or community effort are mobilized, either through their conversion into public revenues as taxes, fees, betterment contributions, and other fiscal means, or through the provision of on-site land improvements that benefit the community. The reference to increments in value rather than in land price indicates that the increment or appreciation is often assessed according to estimated values rather than realized market prices. In a few cases, such as CEPACs in Brazil, the land value increment is revealed in market transactions through public auctions.

The working definition of value capture encompasses three important components. First, it refers exclusively to increments in the value of the land. Thus, when assessing property appreciation, the productivity gains or changes in values associated with the value of the buildings are not to be charged or captured.

Second, different legal frameworks may interpret how community effort generates land value increments in various ways, over and above any explicit public intervention in the form of a financial investment or an administrative action applied to land uses. Land readjustment schemes, for instance, may be promoted by a nonpublic entity with the resulting land value increment shared by the participants according to criteria established in advance.

Third, the term *mobilization of the land value increment* is proposed rather than public appropriation. The latter term refers to the conversion of land value increments resulting from a community effort into taxes, fees, and the like to be spent on services and public investments. However, the community at large can benefit more directly when the process is applied to a set of landowners who are both contributors to and beneficiaries of the land value increment, as in the case of large-scale urban operations.

Although the general rule is that actions by entities other than the landowner, primarily the public sector or broader societal changes, affect most land value increases, certain actions taken directly by private developers may enhance the value of their land. A common yet fallacious allegation of privately generated land value increment is made when a private agent develops a high-end gated community in a low-priced area, since this new project will dramatically enhance the value of the developed plots. An argument can be made that the capacity to create unanticipated externalities that can be internalized in each plot should be appropriated in part by the investor or developer as a legitimate gain, just as certain gains from mergers or other actions are earned by business investors. However, some of the accrued land value increments are not intrinsic to the development itself, but result from conditions already found in the city.

In the case of two identical gated communities, the one located in a city facing strong competition from similar developments would likely generate much lower land value increments than the other one located where no similar alternatives have yet been offered. Thus, a significant component of the willingness to pay for attributes of the gated community (e.g., location, amenities) corresponds to the willingness to pay for attributes found in other parcels in the city, just as the value of a single plot is determined according to its differential attributes compared to other plots. In other words, the value of the internalized externalities is affected by the gated community's overall value in the city as a whole.

THE GROWING POPULARITY OF VALUE CAPTURE POLICIES AND TOOLS

Value capture legislation or applications can be found in local jurisdictions in most Latin American countries, even when no national legislation exists. Several factors account for this growing popularity of value capture as part of the urban planner's toolbox.

Decentralization

The trend toward fiscal decentralization—a process accompanied by restraints on traditional revenue transfers together with greater fiscal autonomy and more responsibility for service provision—encourages municipalities to expand their own statutory sources of revenue. Many administrations are placing higher importance on local sales taxes and other fees, while a few are looking at means to improve the performance of the property tax (De Cesare 2012). Given the widespread unpopularity of this tax, however, some jurisdictions view value capture

as an attractive alternative. Even small municipalities in the Brazilian state of Paraná, which are losing population and consequently their share of transfers from the state or federal level, have resorted to betterment contributions as a complementary source of revenue (Pereira 2012).

Urban Planning and Management

The shift of emphasis from comprehensive planning to city management over the last few decades has created an environment more receptive to the application of instruments based on negotiation and relaxation of existing norms (Vainer 2000). Local planning officials find greater flexibility in tools that tend to be applied on a project or site basis as opposed to traditional, citywide fiscal instruments.

This trend has been coupled with the growing presence of private investors eager to promote specific land development projects. While developers would always prefer not to be charged extra fees, they are often willing to surrender a share of the gains from additional building rights, as in various linkage programs and urban operations in Brazil. Some practitioners, especially critics of comprehensive urban planning, find value capture tools useful as a strategy to make large-scale urban development more viable, or as a guarantee of the sustainability of individual projects. This view has shaped recent urban development throughout the region, and in São Paulo in particular.

Redemocratization and Increasing Social Awareness

Redemocratization in many Latin American countries has raised the level of popular participation, increased the politicization of social inequalities (the so-called social debt accumulated from the former authoritarian and dictatorial regimes), and challenged governments to address the roots of these

Many citizens participated in Brazil's third Conference of the Cities in 2007.

inequities. Social demands in turn put pressure on local officials for increased public spending. Many value capture initiatives are associated with, and motivated by, the mobilization of new and more flexible funds to finance special social programs.

In the land policy realm, value capture has been associated with many constitutional and legislative reforms that redefine property rights, obligations (often embodying the social function of property and the right to housing, or more generally the "right to the city"), and the ability of public administrations to redistribute the benefits and costs of urbanization. These ideas contradict the pervasive and traditional mode of state intervention in Latin America, typified by the phrase "socialization of costs and privatization of benefits."

Neoliberal Agendas and Privatization

The notion that the beneficiaries of a publicly provided benefit (potential free riders) should compensate society is easily accepted by proponents of mainstream economics as adhering to marginal principles of price efficiency. The dissemination and influence of the so-called neoliberal agenda has paradoxically helped reduce ideological resistance to value capture.

Tolerance of free riders is certainly not a neo-liberal idea. In 1974 a mayor of the Providence Commune ratified by General Augusto Pinochet's dictatorship in Chile (the epitome of laissez-faire practices in Latin America) argued publicly that value capture was indispensable to urban planning proposals. In this high-income area, a charge was proposed on landowners benefiting from the construction of a new avenue (named 11 of September, honoring the date of the military coup). The proposal was later blocked by the finance minister, but the construction of a subway line under the avenue had required some expropriations that were compensated well below the appreciation values anticipated by the landowners, thus indirectly benefiting the community in any case (Cáceres and Sabatini 2002).

Privatization, in turn, has set the stage for the development of more flexible public interventions, public-private partnerships, and direct negotiations over land uses and regulations. Significant examples are the release of public land into the private land market and better coordination between real estate and public sector interests to promote new areas for urban development.

Influence of Multilateral Agencies

Value capture ideas have been promoted by multilateral agencies stressing user fees and cost recovery of public investments as good practices. For example, explicit concerns with value capture can be found in the Vancouver Declaration (UN-Habitat 1976), which includes Recommendation D3.b:

> *The unearned increment resulting from the rise in land values resulting from change in use of land, from public investment or decision, or due to general growth of the community must be subject to appropriate recapture by public bodies (the community), unless the situation calls for other additional measures such as new patterns of ownership, the general acquisition of land by public bodies.*

More recently UN-Habitat has organized conferences to understand how value capture is practiced in different regions and has made more use of value capture tools (Sietchiping 2011). The World Bank also has commissioned papers on alternative tools for financing infrastructure (Blackburn and Dowall 1991) and on ways to unlock land values to finance urban infrastructure (Peterson 2009). The Inter-American Development Bank organized a seminar in January 2013 to identify what is being done in Latin America and the need for further research on ways it could adopt value capture tools in their funding practices in the region.

Pragmatic Considerations

With the macroeconomic stabilization of most economies in the region, the dramatic reduction of chronic inflation gave transparency to windfalls otherwise disguised as nonoperational real estate gains. In highly inflationary regimes land value increments are often embedded in mark-ups reflecting expectations of price increases. Opportunism is another motivation behind some attempts by public officials to implement value capture policies, since the value that is captured can be directed to funds or projects not covered by regular taxes and other own revenues, thus leveraging the local authority's discretionary expenditure capacity.

Value capture often emerges as a pragmatic substitute for the poor performance record of property tax collections and other instruments. This option is especially attractive when, due to active political opposition, a local administration finds it cannot increase its own fiscal revenues, let alone carry out investment plans for social programs.

CHAPTER 2
International and Latin American Experiences

Value capture policies and tools are by no means limited to Latin America. A long trajectory of international experiences has demonstrated that defraying at least part of the cost of urbanization by using the land value increment created in the process is feasible and practical (Hagman and Misczynski 1978; Smolka and Furtado 2001; Vejarano 2007; Peterson 2009; Muñoz Gielen 2010; Alterman 2012; Ingram and Hong 2012; Walters 2012; Furtado and Acosta 2013).

HISTORICAL PRECEDENTS

The use of valorization to construct new roads and maintain aqueducts has been documented as early as the Roman Empire, but it probably existed before then since it is based on the understanding that if you get benefits, you should pay for them (Villamil 2000). Arguments calling for fees to be imposed on landowners benefiting from some type of public investment (roads, bridges, and the like) can be found in Portugal and Spain in the 1500s, and their application in Latin America has been traced back to 1607 in Mexico (Reyes 1980).

England used valorization around the year 1650 to build canals along the Lea and Thames Rivers, and in 1801 the House of Lords authorized a betterment levy for urban development purposes. France began to use valorization in 1672 to build parks, roads, and bridges, and a special type of

The Bridge of the Commons was built in 1809 in Bogotá, Colombia, using a form of betterment contribution.

© KAMILOKARDONA/WIKIMEDIA COMMONS

valorization was also used after World War I to reconstruct the country. In Italy it was used as early as the seventeenth century to enlarge parks and to make improvements in the city of Florence (Reyes 1980).

Elsewhere around the world, Japan relied extensively on land readjustment instruments to promote urbanization following World War II, and these tools are also applied in South Korea and Finland (Hong and Needham 2007). Taiwan has had an explicit tax on land value increments since the times of Dr. Sun Yat-Sen, the founding father of China's republic, inspired by his Equalization of Land Rights principles. Leasing systems on public lands capture value through regular contract adjustments in Hong Kong and still play an important role in various cities in the Netherlands, especially Rotterdam.

Gains associated with rights provided in partial or comprehensive plans have been used to fund new urbanized areas in many European countries, such as England's right to tax the increase in value caused by the rezoning of land and France's *Plafond Légal de Densité*, whereby charges were levied for building rights over and above a certain baseline. In Spain, municipalities capture part of the value increase in urban extension areas by requiring landowners to cede between 5 and 15 percent of the serviced building plots to the municipality. In addition, landowners must provide the land needed for infrastructure, pay the related costs for service provision, and pay the overhead costs and a profit margin (Muñoz Gielen 2010).

Since the 1970s, about 25 percent of jurisdictions in the United States have imposed impact fees on developers to fund the provisions of infrastructure improvements paid for by the community (Lawhon 2003). In Florida, for example, over US$2 billion was collected in fiscal years 2005–2006, with the fees accounting for more than 5 percent of the revenues in 48 counties. In the state's large counties with over one million inhabitants, such as Orange County, these fees accounted for 28 percent of local revenues (Burge 2010).

Notwithstanding growing concerns with lack of access to serviced land by the urban poor, the underlying principle of paying for urbanization costs using the associated land value increment has not been widely adopted in most parts of the third world. Strong market-based countries like the United States and Canada have actually been more active in recovering the unearned income resulting from land rents than countries south of the U.S. border, although in a less explicit form (Smolka and Amborski 2007).

ENABLING LEGISLATION

The most comprehensive and systematic examples of value capture legislation in Latin America are found in Colombia's Law 388 of 1997 (*Ley 388 de 1997*) and Brazil's Statute of the City of 2001 (*Estatuto da Cidade*). Although both resulted from a long period of trial and error with other legislation, they differ significantly. The Colombian process has been markedly top down, whereas in Brazil social mobilization associated with the urban reform movement played a significant role in the post-redemocratization reform of the Constitution in 1988 and other initiatives.

Colombia's Law 388, in Article 73, introduces the notion that public actions that improve urban land uses, including the associated air space, give the public the right to participate in the resulting land value increments (*plusvalías*). The law's Article 74 specifies the sources of these benefits as the conversion of rural land to urban uses, changes in zoning and density, and the rate of land occupation. Article 79 states that local or district councils may share from

Varied types of buildings illustrate changing land uses over time in Rambla Mahatma Gandhi, Montevideo, Uruguay.

30 to 50 percent of the *plusvalías*. The law includes other provisions relating to value capture, such as permitting the public auction of idle land to be used for social housing after proper notification of the owners; the right of the public to have the first option to buy the land; the public acquisition of land at prices listed before the announcement of the project; and the enabling of land readjustment in partial plans.

Brazil's 2001 statute incorporates many principles relevant to value capture that were established previously in Article 182 of the 1988 Constitution. They include the social function of property as reflected in the application of progressive property taxation on vacant land; the separation of building rights from land ownership rights; new tools like the Consortia for Urban Operations that allow special treatment for recognized stakeholders (owners, residents, users, and private investors) to redevelop large areas; the right of first option to municipal governments to acquire land; and the use of transfer of development rights.

In regard to administrative actions, such as charges on development rights, the Colombian law has had more influence on subsequent legislation in other countries of the region than the Brazilian statute, which contemplates a broader scope and calls for capturing up to 100 percent of the land value increment. This difference is likely due to the language and imprint of Spanish legislation in Colombia, whereas Brazil was more influenced by the French precedent.

Several other countries have passed national legislation enhancing the power of governments to mobilize land value increments. Uruguay's 2008 Law (*Ordenamiento Territorial y Desarrollo Sostenible*) establishes the principle of equitable distribution among public and private actors of charges and benefits from the urbanization process, including the capture of values generated in land use planning and development. Its Article 46 contains an explicit value capture provision authorizing municipalities to share in the higher land value increments resulting from their interventions.

Citizens support a congressional debate over the promulgation of new land development laws for the Province of Buenos Aires, Argentina.

The instrument, referred to as a return on valorization, is set at a minimum of 15 percent of the increment resulting from public actions. This charge on the full additional property value represents an ingenious way to bypass the difficulties of calculating the land value appreciation resulting from public actions since the 15 percent figure is an estimate of the average share of land value in the final price of the property.

The municipality of Montevideo has been applying an instrument referred to as compensatory price since 2001, thus even before the national act was passed. It charges 10 percent on the value of the entire property or up to 10 percent when developments are in strategic areas or are part of special plans. In 2011 the city collected only US$3.8 million from this source, about 2.5 percent of its total investment budget of about US$150 million. However, some new developments, such as FORUM in the Puerto del Buceo area and a new shopping center (Shopping Nuevo Centro), are expected to generate about US$5 million each.

The smaller municipality of Maldonado in the state of Punta de Este, Uruguay, by contrast, has collected US$4.5 million, or more than 11 percent of its US$40 million worth of investments (Mendive 2013).

Ecuador's 2010 COOTAD (*Código Orgánico de Organización Territorial, Autonomía y Descentralización*) established a 10 percent tax on land value increments when properties are transferred, a deduction of *plusvalías* in expropriations for social housing and regularization projects, and an explicit recognition of illicit enrichment with no just cause.

Argentina has had an ongoing congressional debate over national legislation, but Buenos Aires and other municipalities, including Córdoba, Moreno, Morón, Rosario, San Fernando, Trenque Lauquen, and Venado Tuerto, already have concrete and distinct value capture experiences. Ordinance 3808 of 2011 in Tranque Lauquen, one of the 135 small municipalities in the province of Buenos Aires, calls for 12 percent of the plots in new subdivisions at the urban fringe to be transferred to the government for social housing. These areas are over and above the regular obligatory cessions of land for preservation, streets, public facilities, and the like. The fee transfer has been applied to many requests for rezoning (affecting FAR increases from .8 to 1.2 and minimum lot size reductions from 600 to 300 m²) generating for the municipality a sizeable number of plots to be used for social programs.

A progressive Law on Fair Access to Habitat for the Province of Buenos Aires, approved in late 2012, required the contribution of at least 10 percent of the land value increment generated by large urban developments occupying more than 5,000 m²; a 50 percent increase in the property tax on vacant land; a special contribution on plots benefiting from zoning changes; and opportunities to readjust public land for social housing programs.

In general, across all countries in the region and at different times, national or local legislation can be found to include provisions for some form of value capture. A 1940 decree in Honduras, for example, allowed for property owners to pay a third of the cost of paving projects on streets that bordered their properties. In 1976, another decree explicitly authorized the Central District (Tegucigalpa) to collect betterment contributions. This provision was extended in 1984 to the municipality of San Pedro Sula, and in 1987 to all municipalities (Kehew 2002). Costa Rica's Urban Planning Law No. 4240 of 1969 allowed for betterment contributions, and it was later broadened in the reform of 1972. Nicaragua's Municipal Arbitration Plan of 1988 also anticipated use of a betterment contribution.

In the emblematic case of Guatemala, Article 132 in the 1956 Constitution established that property owners who benefited from *plusvalías* as a result of public works were obligated to contribute an amount in proportion to their benefits. This stipu-lation was to be regulated by the Law on the *Plusvalías* Tax and Improvements Fees, which also had language regarding the social character of the benefits accruing to property owners. As with similar initiatives in the region, the project was blocked by strong opposition from landowners and others who characterized it as socialist.

Venezuela, in its 1999 reform of the Bolivarian Constitution, included the possibility for municipalities to charge special contributions for land value increments resulting from changes in land use or density. The municipality of Baruta included in its zoning ordinances for the development of La Naya-Las Manitas and Urbanización Las Mercedes a charge of 5 percent of *plusvalías;* between 2002 and 2010, US$9.4 million was collected from properties in that area (Monserrat Guzman 2010).

Other countries have had varying degrees of success in fully establishing and enforcing their value capture legislation. In Mexico, Article 115 of the 1982 reform of the constitution allows municipalities to collect additional fees (as defined by the states) on certain actions associated with land development (e.g., subdivisions or consolidations), and on improvements that change the value of properties. Fiscal legislation in seven states refers to this tool as a tax on *plusvalías,* although in essence it is a betterment contribution that has not been fully implemented countrywide (Perló Cohen and Zamorano Ruiz 2001).

Local officials often allege their hands are tied and they avoid taking action, even when they actually are permitted to apply many value capture instruments. This situation resonates throughout the region where principles (sometimes in explicit value capture parlance) established administratively or by law are essentially ignored in practice, or at best are implemented partially or selectively in a few jurisdictions.

APPLICATIONS TO PUBLIC LANDS

The disparity between principle and practice is illustrated by the challenges surrounding the acquisition, retention, and disposition of public lands. Each step in the process is heavily regulated, often with an explicit value capture rationale, in virtually all jurisdictions in the region, though only a few places have a specific policy tool in place. Public authorities acquire land relying on eminent domain, expropriations, direct purchases, or another means. Each approach has some concern regarding the "just price," usually as prescribed by law but often equated to the current commercial price (Rabello de Castro 2006).

Public Acquisition of Land

The recently enacted Decree 9050 of June 15, 2012 in Venezuela seeks to determine the just price of properties in cases of emergency expropriations for housing and settlements. Article 2 establishes that the just price is to be based on the value of the property's most recent acquisition. If that occurred within the same year, the base value would be the previous registered transaction. Article 3 states that the value would be updated according to the average price indexes and nominal interest rates defined by the central bank. Most important, it adds that in no case may the calculation of the just price consider any influence or impact generated by planned public or private investments in the immediate area, nor the expected returns derived from uses established by urban land use norms and regulations. It also establishes that the just price cannot consider the current market value.

Colombia is one of the few countries where an explicit tool has been designed to address the calculation of public land acquisition prices: the Project Announcement (*Anuncio del Proyecto*) included in Law 388 of 1997. Under this powerful provision the commercial value (for compensatory purposes) cannot include the increment attributed to the planned project itself. In practice this condition freezes the acquisition land price to its level prior to the announcement of the project, and therefore is an expedient instrument to capture the land value increment that otherwise would accrue to the landowner, or to reduce the land cost that the local administration would pay for its own urban development projects.

For example, the city of Bogotá managed to acquire 62 hectares of land for the Nuevo Usme project in 2000 at about US$8.5/m^2 and in 2010 about 80 hectares at US$3.5/m^2 on average, when the typical commercial value of similar land sold by pirate subdividers was rarely below US$20/m^2 (Pinilla 2013). One of the largest landowners in the project area stated in his appeal against the administrative expropriation that his land was worth US$50/m^2. In fact, the land was acquired at below US$2.50/m^2 in 2000.

Land Banking

It is generally understood that the stock of public land should be used diligently and strategically according to socioeconomic and urban development priorities. Land banking is one way to acquire large tracts to be held for relatively long periods of time to better control the use of the land, to prevent speculation, and through their ultimate sale or lease to capture for the community any increase in land value resulting from public or market actions. Public officials frustrated with land market regulations are often seduced by this idea, but its effective implementation in Latin America has been limited for several reasons: lack of resources; higher short-term priorities for scarce public funds; thorny legal procedures for acquiring land; the local influence of strong private landowning interests; the disruptive impacts

© CLAUDIO ACIOLY

Many sections of Brazil's coastal land, as in Copacabana Beach in Rio de Janeiro, are publicly owned and leased to private users.

of high inflation on land prices; and poor management practices.

Again, although it is an almost universally approved urban policy, only a few Latin American countries have applied land banking effectively. Mexico has used this approach most systematically through its *Reservas Territoriales* program (Brito 1998). In perhaps the most interesting application, the municipality of Aguascalientes managed a successful program to prevent the establishment of informal settlements during the 1980s and 1990s. The administration acquired land through expropriation and other negotiations to provide an alternative to informal occupations while at the same time imposing sanctions on subdivisions offered by pirate developers (Jiménez Huerta 2013). The program was discontinued, however, when an opposing political party took over the administration.

In general, land banking has a convoluted history in Latin America, since publicly owned assets are easily disposed of by the clientelistic practices of politicians, given away for questionable projects, or invaded by low-income families who find it easier

(and more secure) to occupy public than private lands.

Land Leasing

A significant amount of public land is disposed under leasing concessions to private users who pay a fee for the right to occupy the land for a given time period, often in perpetuity. This type of lease is widely used in the region, especially in coastal areas. Residents in the Copacabana beach neighborhood in Rio de Janeiro, for instance, technically do not own their properties, just the right to use and transfer them. Fees for the right of use tend to be set at symbolic levels and collection is often ignored. However, when land is transferred, a fee (referred to as a *laudemio*) is charged up to 5 percent of the transacted value.

As in the case of land banking, there is little experience with land leasing as a value capture tool to promote urban development in the region. A notable case is the autonomous fiscal and administrative district of the historic center of Havana, Cuba, which is under the control of the Office of the Historian. Through an operative corporation,

Cia Habaguanex, the office restores buildings to rent, lease, or sell, and also sells special services. A revolving fund, created by the lease payments, tax revenues, and international donations for historic preservation, supplements the 5 percent tax collected on revenues from businesses operating in rehabilitated buildings in the district.

On a somewhat smaller scale the municipality of San Fernando near Buenos Aires created a joint public-private entity that is owned 51 percent by the municipality and 49 percent by CACEL (the Argentinean Chamber of Light Boat Manufacturers). Through a 20-year lease, it administers the concession of a commercial marine park on public riverfront land covering about 5 km². Besides participating in the company's profits, the municipality receives CACEL's annual lease payment and other regular local taxes and fees that generated about US$4 million in revenues over the last six years. Half of these funds have been used to finance social housing units and the upgrading of low-income neighborhoods and the other half to invest in park improvements and public access along the river bank.

SELECTED VALUE CAPTURE TOOLS

Over and above the rather eratic application of otherwise ubiquitous institutional provisions affecting public land management, jurisdictions in most countries have devised tools to capture some land value increment resulting from a public intervention. The variety of issues addressed under many institutional circumstances often results in a local interpretation being given to the tools, which makes an objective assessment of their use very difficult.

This report focuses on selected tools that meet the following criteria: innovative and original; most relevant to the urban problem being addressed; representative of multiple jurisdictions; consistent in the application of core principles over time; and effective in terms of the level of impact.

Although value capture instruments are conventionally categorized as taxes, contributions, fees, exactions, and regulatory charges (Smolka and Amborski 2007), here they are organized within three groups:

- taxes and fees, including betterment contributions;
- exactions and other regulatory charges for building rights; and
- a variety of tools used in large urban development projects.

The distinctions are not exclusive, however, because the same tool may embody subtleties that defy classification. The Colombian *Participación in Plusvalías*, for example, can support betterment contributions to recover the cost of public works investments or exactions to capture the increased value resulting from a change in zoning regulations. Moreover, in Colombia this instrument is considered a tribute or fee, but in Brazil a similar instrument that charges for additional building rights (*Outorga Onerosa do Direito de Construir*, OODC) is not. Under Brazilian law building rights are not considered an inherent component of the real estate property right but rather a way of using the property bestowed by the public (Rabello de Castro 2012).

Similarly, in most uses of exactions where the generating factor is flexibility in land use norms, the compensation is often made through public works to support the permitted new uses. Although the revenues collected by all of these kinds of tools are included in the overall municipal budget, typically managed by the local treasury secretary, in some cases the value capture proceeds take the form of in-kind compensation.

CHAPTER 3
The Property Tax and Betterment Contributions

© BORRERO OCHOA Y ASOCIADOS LTDA., BOGOTÁ

Property taxes, contributions, and fees are typically levied on existing land values or on increments to those values due to changed conditions or land uses. Revenues tend to be used to defray investment or maintenance costs for public works, transportation, and other infrastructure.

THE PROPERTY TAX

Any tax on land value, typically levied only on private property, is a form of value capture in so far as much of the land value results from accumulated public actions and investments. It follows that the property tax captures some value since the tax rate applies to both buildings and land. This point has led some to wrongly claim the imposition of double taxation when a charge on building rights is added to the regular property tax. The Brazilian Supreme Court has ruled that the charge on additional building rights (OODC) is not a tax but rather a charge imposed on the use of "additional building rights that are not part of the owner's assets but a public good that belongs to the city as a whole" (Rabello de Castro 2012, 18).

Some observers consider value capture a replacement for land value taxation at the margin. But because property taxes are not usually associated with any particular public intervention, others question whether they should be recognized as an instrument of value capture.

In making their decision on where to reside, individuals often consider the bundle of services offered by a jurisdiction in return for a particular property tax payment. The

Avenue Boyacava in Bogotá, Colombia, is a north-south route passing through residential and commercial areas. This public work collected about US$320 million in betterment contributions.

celebrated Tiebout hypothesis suggests that the property tax can be seen as a user charge because taxpayers can choose which jurisdiction offers the highest level of benefits in exchange for a particular tax rate (Fischel 2005). This hypothesis of "voting with your feet" is weaker in Latin America than in the United States because fiscal autonomy and the share of property taxes in local revenues are minimal.

The property tax is, economically speaking, a combination of one of the worst taxes— the part that is assessed on real estate improvements . . . and one of the best taxes— the tax on land or site value.

William Vickrey (1999), Nobel Prize in Economics, 1996

It has some bearing, though, on the debates surrounding certain wealthy neighborhoods seeking more legal autonomy, such as the arguments raised by residents of Barra da Tijuca in Rio de Janeiro in the 1990s, or as a criteria to redistribute a centrally collected property tax among municipalities in a fragmented context such as the metropolitan area of Santiago, Chile. In both situations residents claimed that their tax share was higher than the services they received. On the other hand, Bogotá's voluntary 10 percent supplemental tax payment allows taxpayers to choose how their additional contributions should be spent from among 10 publicly provided city services, thus offering an opportunity for local taxes to be treated as direct user payments (Pinilla and Florián 2011).

Land Value Taxation
The land value tax presents, in theory, many desirable features compared to the conventional land-plus-building property tax. Its

burden falls entirely on landowners, it does not distort economic decisions in regard to land use, and it does not generate the excess burden (deadweight loss) common to most taxes (Oates and Schwab 2009). At the same time, it has a bearing on value capture because public expenditures for infrastructure and service improvements, norms and regulations affecting land uses, and other locational attributes (externalities in general) are all fully capitalized in land values (as opposed to buildings that tend to be valued on their intrinsic attributes).

The same principles that solidly ground land value taxation in economic theory apply in principle to value capture, since public benefits are ultimately capitalized as land value increments. Observed land prices can be perceived as either the accumulation of all land value increments over time or the present (or discounted) value of a stream of land-based services expected to be obtained in the future.

In its more radical version that advocates full confiscation of all rents related to public actions, the land value tax would ultimately eliminate the need for any additional value capture tool (George 1992). It should be clear that a full tax on such land rents would result in its market value dropping dramatically as the present value of the expected flow of future rents net of taxes would also be small. The landowner nevertheless would still be taxed periodically for an amount corresponding to the total rental value of his land.

A system in which the property tax falls entirely on the land value has few precedents. The most significant experience can be found in Baja California in Mexico, especially in Mexicali (Perló Cohen and Zamorano 1999). In a recent study, López Padilla and Gómez Rocha (2013) found that the shift to a land value tax base in Mexicali improved tax collections by about 400 percent over the last 20 years. By 2005 Mexicali out-performed comparable municipalities with conventional tax bases, or at least matched well-known high performers such as the much richer (in per capita income) city of Hermosillo. In addition, there are indications that Mexicali expanded at a higher density, as would be expected from theory.

In spite of these desirable features, tax authorities in Latin America tend to favor the conventional property tax on land and buildings due to the ease of observing and recording market transactions, as opposed to the more roundabout land value assessment methods for built-up areas. They have also been reluctant to implement land value taxation in part because it could be regressive for the large numbers of low-income families for whom the land represents a higher share of their property value than their precarious housing structures (De Cesare et al. 2003).

Temporary Property Tax Rate Increase

Value capture may also be associated with a temporary rate increase in property taxes, as when an additional charge is applied for financing large-scale urban infrastructure that benefits all residents directly or indirectly in proportion to their property values.

For example, to pay for a new 40 km subway line in Buenos Aires that would double the existing capacity, Law 23.514 of 1987 created a special fund with a 5 percent addition to property taxes from all city residents, plus another 2.4 percent surcharge for those residents within 400 meters of the stations (Cuenya et al. 2003). In 2012 revenues accruing to this fund amounted to about US$750 million. However, other revenue sources from expressway tolls, betterment contributions, and automobile licenses generated four times that amount. In general, the property tax in Buenos Aires accounts for only about 8 percent of total city revenues, second to the gross local income tax, and it is charged at rates that increase progressively according to bands of assessed property values.

BETTERMENT CONTRIBUTIONS

A betterment contribution (known as a special assessment in the United States) is a charge or fee imposed on owners of selected properties to defray the cost of a public improvement or service from which they specifically benefit (Borrero Ochoa 2011; Borrero Ochoa et al. 2011). It is not only the oldest but likely the most consistently used value capture instrument, with cases since the early nineteenth century in countries such as Argentina, Brazil, and Colombia.

In Bogotá, the Bridge of the Commons was built in 1809 using a form of betterment contribution, although the first specific national legislation was not approved until 1887. It was established to distribute the costs of dike projects to those benefiting from their construction. "Subsequent legislation in 1921 authorized the use of assessments in rural areas for flood and drainage projects. By 1936, Law 195 allowed cities hard-pressed to find infrastructure financing mechanisms to use special assessment financing to supplement existing resources" (Walker 2000, 114).

In Brazil, such a levy was introduced constitutionally in 1934, but it had appeared in a 1921 decree of the then Federal District (Rio de Janeiro) as a real estate valorization contribution. In 1909, São Paulo established a law that the city council would only approve new streets proposed by private interests if they would cover half of the pavement costs, and in the 1920s a pavement fee was introduced (Sandroni 2001).

Almost all Latin American countries now have national laws that permit some version of a valorization fee or charge to enable the public sector to capture the increments of land value directly associated with public investments (Manon and Macon 1977). Even in El Salvador, where full property taxes have not yet been introduced, the constitution allows for the collection of special contributions (Lungo and Oporto 1998). In Chile, where value capture issues are still viewed skeptically, contributions for road pavement programs have been promoted since 1927 and have been defined under law since 1953 (Cáceres and Sabatini 2002).

Significant Variations in Performance

In spite of the betterment levy's apparent universality, it still plays a negligible role in most jurisdictions' finances, as it typically accounts for much less than 1 percent of own local revenues. In Mexico, for example, it represents no more than .42 percent of municipal revenues (Pérez Torres and Acosta Peña 2012); in Brazil in 2011 it represented

.25 percent of all fiscal revenues and 6.8 percent of all property-related tributes (Afonso et al. 2010); and in Rosario, Argentina, it accounted for .30 percent of own revenues (Alvarez 2009).

Some notable municipal outliers are in Colombia, where in 1968, at the height of its use, the betterment contribution was responsible for 45 percent of all local public expenditures in Medellín; in the early 1980s, 30 percent of Cali's expenditures; and in 1993, 24 percent of Bogotá's local revenues (Furtado 2000; Jaramillo 1998). After periods of neglect in Bogotá its use resurged in recent years, with about US$1 billion worth of public works being funded by the instrument (table 3.1).

A lesser known outlier is the municipality of Cuenca, Ecuador, which over the last 10 years issued 1,800 contracts for public works projects and collected almost US$200 per capita, much higher than Bogotá's US$150 in the same period. Cuenca's US$25 per capita fees collected in the single year of 2010 (totaling US$12.4 million) also far surpassed those of Bogotá in any single year. Cuenca also excelled in terms of performance, with 90 percent of households making their contributions in less than four years, 95 percent of the projects collecting 60 percent in betterment contributions, and only 3 percent of contributors found to be noncompliant.

Collection of betterment contributions is not consistent among countries, or within countries among their jurisdictions or across time. For example, in Mexico, only four states—Coahuila, Estado de México, Sonora, and Zacatecas—account for 86 percent of total national revenues from betterment contributions (Pérez Torres and Acosta Peña 2012). In Ecuador, 74 percent of all betterment contributions are collected in its three largest cities (Cuenca, Quito, and Guayaquil), although they account for only

TABLE 3.1

Charges Collected from Public Works Programs Funded by Betterment Contributions in Bogotá, 1993–2013

Programs	Year of Approval	Date of Charge	US$ (TRM)
Basic Valorization across the City	1993	1993	106,160,600
		Subtotal	106,160,600
Forming the City Program (Formar Ciudad)	1995	1996–1998	351,928,000
	2001	2002	55,931,000
		Subtotal	407,859,000
Agreement 180 of 2005 (modified by Agreement 398 of 2009)	2005	Phase I- 2007 and 2010	319,311,000
		Phase II- 2012	326,108,000
		Phase III- 2014	321,685,000
		Phase IV- 2016	105,000,000
		Subtotal	1,072,000,000
Agreement 451 of 2010 (Master Plan, Zone North)	Ring Road #1 Charges in 2012		220,000,000

Note: TRM represents the conversion rate from Pesos to US$ (millions) at the respective market value in each year during this time period.

Source: Borrero Ochoa et al. (2011).

© DIEGO ERBA

30 percent of the population (Rodríguez and Aulestia 2013).

Pereira (2012) shows for Brazil that although the betterment contribution in the 2000–2010 decade overall was no more than 1 percent of total tributes on properties, the share in Maranhão, one of the poorest states, was over 10 percent. The municipality of Bacabal in this state has per capita GDP of only $1,300, but collected over US$32 per capita—about half of the highest per capita contribution in any city in the country.

By contrast, São Jose dos Pinhais, in the state of Paraná (the sixth richest in Brazil), with a per capita GDP of about $13,000, collected no more than US$12 in betterment contributions per capita. The same study indicates that for the state of Paraná municipal GDP is negatively related to the relative importance of this fee. For the country as a whole, per capita contributions were about US$1.50. Overall in only 667 of the 5,505

Brazilian municipalities did the betterment contribution represent more than 10 percent of all tributes on properties.

Whereas municipal size is an important factor, larger population is associated with higher collections in absolute terms, but lower population is associated with higher collections relative to other local taxes— possibly because the poorest and smallest municipalities collect little from the service sales tax. The share of contributions is 3 percent of total revenue in municipalities with fewer than 10,000 inhabitants, and the share declines as population increases. Over the 2000–2010 decade, no city in Brazil collected as much as Bogotá or Cuenca (figure 3.1). In other words, there is an enormous variance in the use of the instrument among and within countries, and no robust relation between its performance and a particular city's size or wealth, suggesting that politics may be playing an important role in explaining the observed differences.

Parque de la Madre in Cuenca, Ecuador, was funded by about US$5 million in betterment contributions.

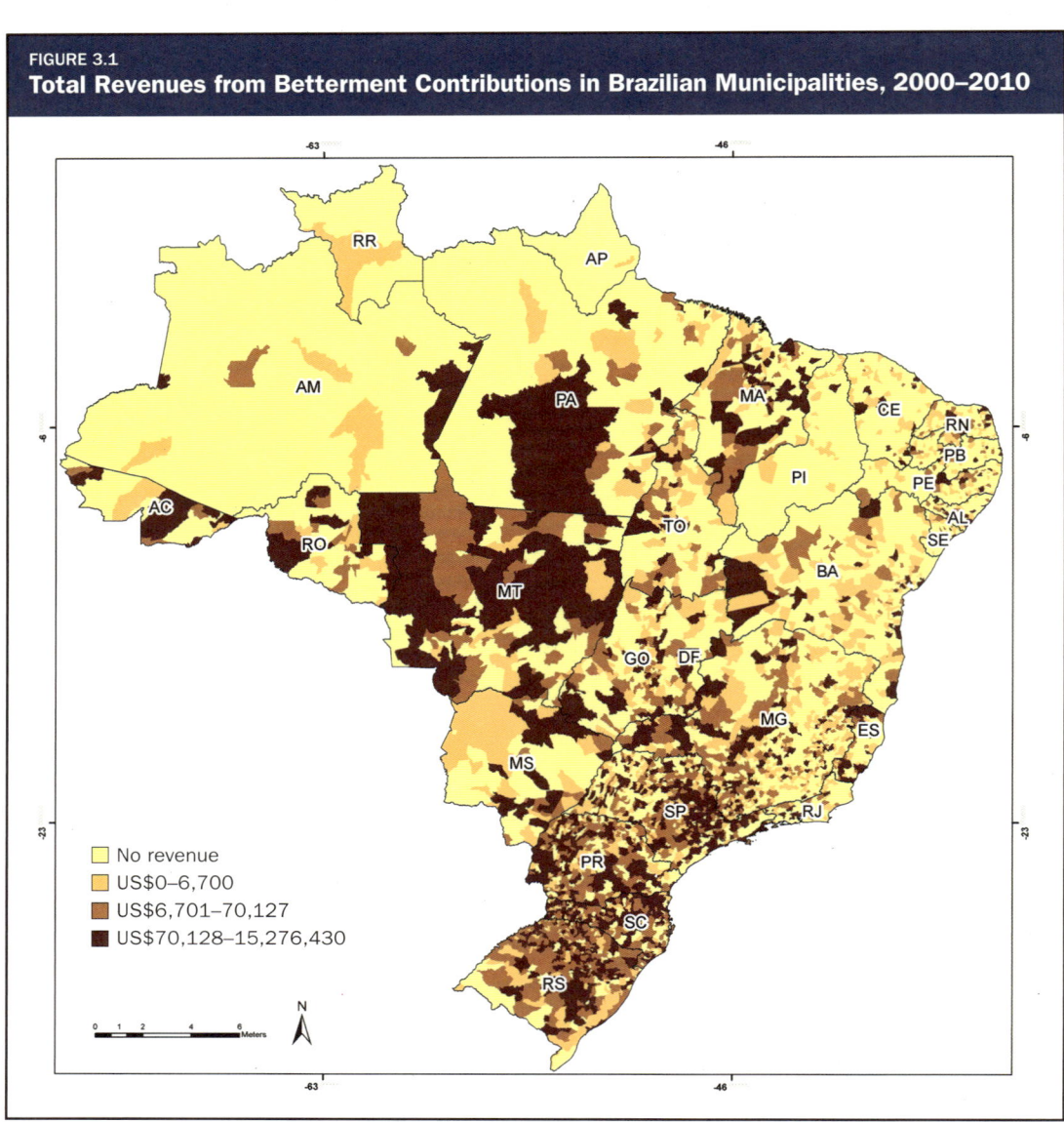

FIGURE 3.1

Total Revenues from Betterment Contributions in Brazilian Municipalities, 2000–2010

Legend:
- No revenue
- US$0–6,700
- US$6,701–70,127
- US$70,128–15,276,430

Notes: 2,890 Brazilian municipalities (52.5 percent of all municipalities) collected some revenue from betterment contributions. The revenues were converted annually to US$. The abbreviations in the map refer to state names.

Source: Pereira (2012).

Considerations in the Application of Betterment Contributions

Although the logic of paying a betterment fee for an investment whose benefits will exceed the fee is straightforward, the application of such an instrument can be quite complicated. This may explain its poor overall performance as a revenue source and why the most successful cases seem to rely on rather arbitrary technical shortcuts to keep it manageable. In practice the estimation of the charge and its distribution among the beneficiaries of a project depends on several important considerations.

The total cost of the project or investment to be recovered

In most places these are the direct costs, but in others some additional charges are imposed, such as in Colombia's Law 25 of 1959 that authorizes adding up to 30 percent to account for items such as the costs of feasibility studies, interest, and administration associated with the public works (García Rojas 2012). In addition to direct costs, the law also includes an allowance for future cost contingencies. The amount to be recovered varies according to the jurisdiction and type of project. Authorities often consider the payment capacity of contributors in the affected area when determining the total amount to be charged.

Most existing legislation limits the amount to be recovered to the lowest value of either the project cost or the land value increment. That is, if the project generates a larger increment than its cost, the latter prevails, whereas if the estimated increment is lower, then only this amount is to be recovered. Some legislation, such as the Brazilian Law of 1967 (no longer in effect), allowed recovery of the full value increment

independently of the project cost. Others, like the Colombian Law 9 of 1989, are more similar to a full-fledged cost-recovery scheme since the charges are collected independently of the benefit.

The practical relevance of these distinctions emerges when distributing the charges among individual properties in the impacted area. In effect, technical imperfections in properly estimating how each property in the defined impacted area will benefit often leads to situations where the charge may be higher than the net benefit for some properties while others receive a lower share of the cost than of the accrued benefit.

The overall land value increment, valorization, or benefits resulting from the investment

In principle any public investment should generate some social improvement, yet not all benefits are necessarily reflected in land

Water is trucked into an informal settlement in Guayaquil, Ecuador.

© MARTIM O. SMOLKA

value increases. For example, in a small city with a precarious water distribution system, an area serviced with piped water has a land value premium that corresponds to areas that must pay higher costs for water provided by trucks. Once water is universalized the land price differentials disappear and, at the same time, no additional land values are added to the land price in the originally unserviced areas. That is, in spite of its great social benefit for the community, the piped water investment may yield an overall net reduction of land values.

This suggests that citywide investments may not be good candidates for betterment fees. For example, public investments thought of as general interest projects may not be desired by neighboring property owners. A study of São Paulo's Ring Road shows that the land value increments vary significantly, and negative values may occur between entry and exit points where the expressway may generate noise and pollution but no clear accessibility benefits (Maciel 2009). Table 3.2 presents varying estimates of the

impacts of Bogotá's Transmilenio bus rapid transit system, obtained from various studies that followed distinct methodologies, illustrating the difficulty of assessing these land value increments.

Definition of the impacted area and identification of all benefited properties

This can be a complex problem since the size of the impacted area (or area of influence) depends on the relevant threshold established for the impact on individual properties and lower thresholds produce larger aggregate impacts. This interdependency is further aggravated if the impact of the project varies among properties according to distance or even over time. When assessing the impacts of bus rapid transit, for example, the properties closest to the stations and the line may actually be valued lower than those in more intermediate locations that still enjoy the convenience of access yet experience less noise and pollution. As distance increases from the stations, the impact progressively

TABLE 3.2
Studies of Bogotá's TransMilenio Bus Rapid Transit (BRT) System and Property Values

Study	Method or Measurement	Result
Rodríguez and Targa (2004)	Rents on 494 multifamily residential properties in a 1.5 km area of influence surrounding two TransMilenio corridors.	A premium of 6.8 to 9.3 percent was found for every 5 minutes of walking time closer to a BRT station.
Muñoz-Raskin (2006)	Values of 130,692 new multifamily properties provided by the Bogotá Department of Housing and Control from 2001 to 2004.	Properties within the immediate proximity of feeder lines (0–5 minute walk) were valued higher than those requiring a 5–10 minute walk. High-value properties were valued even higher if they were close to a feeder line, but the effect was the opposite for trunk lines.
Mendieta-López and Perdomo-Calvo (2007)	Assessed property values from cadastral data in 2007 for 1,547 properties within 1 km of TransMilenio.	Property prices increased between 12 and 38 percent, depending on the distance to the BRT at 5-minute increments in walking time to a station.
Perdomo-Calvo et al. (2007)	Analysis of 304 residential properties and 40 commercial properties to compare asking prices in two zones, one with and one without BRT access.	Mixed results, with most comparisons yielding statistically insignificant results. In only one case at standard levels of confidence, a premium of 22 percent for residential properties with BRT access was found.
Rodríguez and Mojica (2008)	Single-family properties at 1 km from the system network and local changes in land value from 2001 to 2006.	Premium between 15 and 20 percent, before inauguration; no evidence of increments along the corridor that had no station but is now serviced by an extension.

Source: Adapted from Rodríguez and Mojica (2008).

BORRERO OCHOA Y ASOCIADOS LTDA., BOGOTÁ

recedes to zero. The rate of perceived decline in benefit with distance may not be constant (Rodríguez and Targa 2004; Flores 2011).

Again in practice the problem is resolved by the application of known, fixed factors drawn from past comparable project contexts, as for example the long-standing practice for street paving projects of simply identifying the beneficiaries as those properties within 500 meters of the project, or for subway expansions, properties within a 600 meter impact radius around a station.

The criteria to distribute the charge among beneficiaries

In principle charges should not be equal for otherwise similar properties with different degrees of access to public works benefits, such as their relative physical location. Additional adjustments can be made according to the size, frontage, or position of the property, for example by applying a factor to accommodate corner properties compared to those within a block or with other unique attributes.

Two primary methods are used to distribute the charge among the individual benefitted properties: the method of factors and the method of double valuation. The first describes the individual physical plot with a series of known or predetermined attributes to calculate a score for each plot. These attributes may include the distance to the public works, built-up area, density, number of retail stores, quality of the building, and the use of the property (industrial, commercial, residential, or charitable). In Colombia the strata of the neighborhood is scored according to its access to urban infrastructure and services as well as socioeconomic attributes of the occupants. All such scores are used to determine the charges (Borrero Ochoa 2011).

A road interchange at Street 100 and Avenue 15 in a high-income area of Bogotá was funded by betterment contributions.

© DIEGO ERBA

The intersection of San Martin and Córdoba streets in Rosario, Argentina, was remodeled for pedestrian use with partial payments from betterment contributions.

The second method relies on the application of impact factors from past experience with comparable situations, typically obtained from hedonic econometric estimations of the effects of relevant property attributes—that is, estimations of land value appreciation from comparable types of projects, interventions, and impacted areas.

This is illustrated by the estimation provided by Chulipa (2007) in the city of Osorio in the state of Rio Grande do Sul in Brazil to forecast the likely impact of a pavement program to be funded by the World Bank. Using parameters obtained from estimations of other plots in the city, the plot distance from the central business district or a subcenter, and the location with respect to the new paved area, the study found a unit value of US$30.72 for plots adjacent to paved areas and US$25.78 for those without such access. A 19 percent rate of appreciation was applied to plots that would benefit from the paving. Relying on original cadastral values for all plots, an overall estimate could be determined for all locations affected by the project.

These two methods are not very different since the parameters are (or should be) obtained from similar hedonic functions. In both methods interpolations of estimated values are made to generate so-called iso-beneficiary zones, that is, homogeneous zones where the same rate is applied to all plots in the area.

Other more arbitrary procedures are sometimes used to distribute the added value of public works, as illustrated for the city of Rosario, Argentina (Alvarez 2009). Plots located within the closest 50 percent of the influence zone absorbed 35 percent of the cost, those in the 50–80 percent influence zone received 24.5 percent, and those in the 80–100 percent zone (estimated originally as 500 meters from each side of the pavement) absorbed 10.5 percent, with the remaining 30 percent of the cost taken up by the public entity.

The payment schedule for the charges

Finally, the payment schedules also vary significantly among jurisdictions in different countries. For example, Colombia imposes the total charge for small projects or a first installment before the investment begins, but Brazil collects payments only upon completion of the project, allowing for a grace period, and then up to five years for full payment. In Cuenca, Ecuador, the payment period can last up to seven years. Installments are also typically limited to a percentage of the fiscal value of the benefited property (e.g., 3 percent in Rosario, Argentina) or to a percentage of the annually collected property tax (90 percent in Brazil and limited to five years).

Contributions Backing Third-Party Loans

Some successful cases of local public investment funding involve input from extra-municipal entities to help repay a loan or for pay-as-you-go financing with schemes grounded in betterment contributions. Some examples are loans provided by the Inter-American Development Bank (IADB) to San Pedro Sula, Honduras, since 1985; and the Paraná-Urbano programs in the state of Paraná, Brazil, in the 1990s through its financial agency Paranacidade (originally funded by the IADB; Goelzer and Saad 1999; Pereira 2012). These initiatives include a capacity-building program, since many small local jurisdictions receiving loans are unfamiliar with such instruments. In Honduras, most of these IADB projects after 2001 were for local sanitary sewer infrastructure, and one was to rehabilitate a school (Kehew 2002).

More recently the case of the *Co-responsabilidade para el Bien Vivir* promoted by the Ecuadorian Bank offers access to subsidized credit to municipalities willing to increase their fiscal effort (in essence, a betterment contribution) as charges associated with the urban infrastructure investments funded by the bank's credit line. This program resulted in an increase in municipal contributions of 67 percent, from US$4.9 million to US$8.2 million, allowing these municipalities to access over US$20 million in credit. The program focused on the 112 municipalities with populations over 20,000, but excluded the three largest cities of Ecuador; 82 of these municipalities adhered to the program, indicating that people will pay increases in local tributes that are linked to greater investment in public works.

Are Betterment Contributions Anti-Poor?

It is often argued that it is unfair to charge the urban poor who benefit from the provision of urban infrastructure and services, for the cost of upgrading or regularization programs. The critique is based on the suggestion that the areas best endowed with urban amenities are typically occupied by high-income families that were not charged when these services were originally provided. Thus it would be unfair to impose charges on those who receive the publicly provided services later.

Evidence shows that expectations regarding publicly funded future upgrading programs lead to higher markups or premiums on current land prices in irregular or illegal settlements. Charging residents for infrastructure benefits would shift the responsibility for collecting the payment from the subdivider to the government. In other words it is not the case that low-income families cannot pay for certain costs. They are already paying the charge to the subdivider through inflated land prices rather than to the public provider of the services (Smolka and Iracheta 1999).

This point seems to be well understood by many lower-income populations, like those in Lima, Peru, where a successful program featuring some 30 projects used a contributory tool to finance public works in the early 1990s. Low-income beneficiaries met the payments since they represented a guarantee of service. Yet, when the policy was extended to higher-income neighborhoods, it generated such strong resistance that it was ultimately discontinued (Gamarra Huayapa 2008).

The alleged inability of poor urban populations to pay for improved services appears to be a myth. In practice, the strategy of attracting some public intervention to one's neighborhood, even if it means paying some of the costs, is perceived as better than no service at all. The charges must be reasonable, however, because in some cases the policy has been applied in low-income areas not to benefit the occupants, for example, but to justify evictions or force out those who cannot pay for the improvements.

CHAPTER 4
Exactions and Charges for Building Rights

The access road Boulevard Los Próceres in Guatemala City was funded with the *Impacto Vial* instrument.

Actions taken by local planning authorities regarding urban norms and regulations often affect land uses or users, and in turn create direct or indirect land value increments for a single plot or a group of plots. Capturing that increment to benefit society is accomplished through the use of cash or in-kind exactions and other types of charges for the use of building rights.

© MUNICIPALITY OF GUATEMALA CITY, DEPARTMENT OF PUBLIC WORKS

EXACTIONS

Exactions are the most common value capture tool used throughout Latin America. They illustrate how landowners may be compelled to make cash or in-kind contributions to obtain special approvals or permission to develop or build on their land. These contributions may be stipulated through subdivision or development agreements based on a particular norm or expectation, or they may be negotiated on an individual basis.

In-kind exactions require the land developers to set apart some of the land for public facilities, including streets, schools, parks, or environmental conservation areas. The most common example in the region requires the land subdivider to release from 15 to 35 percent of the area for public uses. Though ignored in many lower-income subdivisions on affordability grounds, these contributions are often supported by developers of high-end projects on well-located sites with strong valorization potential. In the municipality of Iribarren, Venezuela, a group of landowners actively agreed to contribute to the implementation of many public works, including a park, to enhance the area.

In a São Paulo case, a developer applied for air rights to build an overpass between a shopping center and a garage in another building across the street. His initial expectation of the exaction amount was US$15,000, but after the negotiation he had to pay US$5 million for these rights, based on the costs estimated by public officials that the shopping center would incur to provide public parking facilities if the overpass was not built.

An important lesson can be drawn from this case: when negotiating for an exaction, its upper limit should include the land value increment resulting from the approved exceptions granted to the project.

In Rio de Janeiro, the municipality required the developer of downtown office towers to renovate nearby historic buildings and build a large tank to store rainwater runoff. In the new expansion area of Barra da Tijuca, land developers were required to extend sewerage trunk lines as part of the agreements to allow construction of new buildings.

Other more ad hoc forms of exactions include those negotiated directly between the developer and the local authorities when a license request is submitted for a project that may generate negative externalities in the form of traffic congestion, as in Guatemala, or that modifies existing buildings or land use norms and regulations, as in Córdoba, Argentina.

Mitigating Road Traffic Impacts in Guatemala

An instrument known as *Impacto Vial* has been devised in Guatemala whereby the responsibility for road improvements is shifted to private developers for investments that otherwise would be borne by the public. When a large private development project is submitted for a license, a road traffic study evaluates its impacts on the surrounding community. An infrastructure plan is then designed to mitigate any negative impacts, together with a calculation of the share of the cost the developer should cover.

The work itself is executed by the developer under municipal supervision. Should the cost of the work be higher than the developer's estimated share, the value of the license (about 4.5 percent of total building costs, typically US$230/m^2) is also used to make up for the difference. If both combined sources of funding are insufficient, then other prospective projects in the neighbor-

hood are notified of a charge to cover the budget gap. When the type of required project to mitigate the impacts is still too costly, an earmarked fund is created to collect contributions from other licenses or actual projects in the area.

This process is similar to a cost-recovery betterment contribution since the fee is associated directly with the cost of the public works. It can also be compared to the one-time monetary levy (known as an impact or development fee) that developers in some U.S. counties must remit to the local government in order to obtain a building permit. The differences are that the Guatemalan policy has a narrower scope and that developers make in-kind payments. Typically the payments do not even pass through the municipal coffers because the work is done directly by private agents who are considered more efficient than the public entities. For example, overpasses have been built in four months by private contractors, when they may take from 12 to 16 months if executed by the government.

For large projects with strong negative traffic impacts the mitigating works must be concluded before the inauguration of the development. Since 2006 this instrument has funded nearly all the road construction, totaling more than US$20 million (Municipalidad de Guatemala 2013). It is not considered to be a fee but a mitigation exaction for road traffic impacts.

The Use of Exactions in Argentina

Argentina does not yet have national legislation to support specific means for capturing land value increments, but certain municipalities have some autonomy granted by Article 123 of the National Constitution and have enacted legislation to that effect. Ramon Esteban (2007, 4), former secretary of planning and now a current city councilor in the municipality of San Fernando

© CATALINA MOLLINATI

A new tower in the Portal del Abasto zone of Córdoba, Argentina, required the payment of exactions to obtain a change in building norms.

then soliciting, negotiating, or demanding from them some infrastructure works or improvements in the area of the city where the authorized development takes place.

The city of Córdoba, through Articles 180 to 188 of its province's constitution, exercises its autonomy through its charter that affirms its competence to establish and modify land use norms and regulations. Under this mandate the city has been able to charge for changes in existing building norms and impose an obligation on developers through what is referred to as complementary public works. Under this local legislation the municipality defines the public works to be executed by the developer seeking a change of land use for his own project. As a condition for obtaining the final inspection certificate for the building (a requirement for its registration), the specific public works improvements must be finalized.

An ordinance from the city's Deliberating Council in 2007 determined that changes in land use norms and regulations conveying additional land use benefits to the owner or developer would require a compensation payment in proportion to the benefit. Such payments are provided in-kind in the form of sewer services, drainage, public lighting, or other public works the municipality finds necessary and of comparable cost to the benefit received.

In another form of exaction, the negotiation may involve changes in building norms that place no direct additional burden on existing urban infrastructure and services. In one Córdoba case, a project in the Portal del Abasto zone at the south margin of the Suquía River actually proposed a reduction of the total area to be built from 12,000 to 11,000 m², lowering the FAR from 4.5 to 4.1. However, the project created a new

in the province of Buenos Aires, synthesized the relevance of this tool in the region:

We do not know of municipalities or other Argentinean state entities that act explicitly in relation to value capture. We believe nevertheless that municipalities act informally by either commission or omission. They authorize developments within the legal framework or exempt them of compliance with existing land use norms,

tower of 16 stories that enclosed about 6,300 m² over the allowed height of the original building of seven stories. Whereas the norms limit land coverage to 80 percent, the proposed new tower covers only 64 percent of its plot. After the valorization of the whole project in 2011, the developer was asked to return the equivalent of about US$220,000 to the city for the change granted in land use rights. This contribution was to be paid in-kind in lieu of cash.

CHARGES FOR BUILDING RIGHTS

Instruments in this category are based on the separation of building rights from land ownership rights, which allows the public to recover the land value increment resulting from development rights over and above an established baseline.

Precedent for this instrument is found in Italy, when in 1971 members of the European Economic Commission (EEC) and housing and urban planning experts proposed the separation of building and property rights, suggesting that the former should belong to the community and be granted exclusively by public authorities (Furtado et al. 2010). Other references can be found in Spain, Great Britain, and Colombia; in a memorandum from the 1976 UN-Habitat meeting in Vancouver; and in the U.S. city of Chicago.

However, the French urban reform and land policy of 1975, *Plafond Légal de Densité*, likely had more influence on Brazilian discussions in 1976, when this notion was first raised among urban experts. This law sought to enhance land use control efficiency, reduce social inequalities, and promote more citizen participation in planning. It sets a density ceiling (FAR) of 1 by right for most of the country, with the exception of Paris, where it was fixed at 1.5. Any building rights admitted by local legislation over and above

that limit required payments based on the additional square meters of built area.

Brazilian lawyers, planners, and other urban experts gathered in Embu, in rural São Paulo State, in 1976 to sort out the controversial issues of legally separating land-related rights. Although such a change was originally considered unlawful, a precedent was found in the existing regulations affecting subdivisions that limited building rights by the area granted to the public for roads and other facilities. This approach illustrates how authorities with sufficient political motivation can find creative solutions to otherwise intractable juridical situations.

The first attempt to introduce this concept into a national law in 1983 failed, but it was later included in the Statute of the City in 2001, referencing articles 182 and 183 of Brazil's 1988 Federal Constitution. Since then a mandate has been granted to all municipalities that enables them to charge for any approved building rights over and above a baseline. Technically speaking the additional square footage of the building constitutes public patrimony, and is not to be given away to favor one citizen above another.

Over time the charges levied have evolved from the more ad-hoc manner of exactions, whereby compensation for building rights is negotiated directly with authorities, into one where it is calculated according to predefined criteria applying to any developer seeking additional building rights. In a further extension to more systematic and consistent rules, the policy shifted from extraordinary building rights to any additional right over and above a common baseline, and to all properties in the city or in a well-defined zone based on the master plan.

Linkage Operations

A linkage operation is a particular type of charge that offers permission to build at a higher density or FAR in exchange for the developer contributing toward, or actually providing, affordable housing units or other community benefits. These policies have been used as much in Boston and San Francisco as in São Paulo and Rio de Janeiro (Alterman 1989), though not explicitly in other Latin American countries. In some cases, linkage requirements may be imposed along with exactions, as in the Urban Code approved in Querétaro, Mexico, in 2012 (though not yet implemented), or as mandates within Uruguay's integrated action program (*Programa de Actuación Integrada*).

In the case of São Paulo, the linkage policy evolved from a 1986 zoning law whereby owners of high-valued land occupied by slums could request higher FAR or other uses for the property as long as they built social housing for the original occupants who would be displaced. A municipal decree in 1988 extended the prerogative to owners of land not occupied by slums, thereby establishing a broader linkage program. In 1995 landowners were allowed to pay their compensation in money rather than in social housing itself, since most developers argued that they were not interested in the social housing business. From 1987 to 1998 an additional 857,424 m² of building area was approved by the city of São Paulo in about 328 linkage operations generating US$122.5 million (US$142/ m²) that in turn funded 13,000 social housing units (Sandroni 2011).

In Rio de Janeiro, 100 applications for linkage operations were made to the city's secretariat of urban development through November 2000, after the establishment of Law 16 of 1992 and of regulations in Law 2128 in 1994. Of 36 approved operations (13 from 1993 to 1996 and 23 from 1997 to 2000), 26 were finalized and 22 of these were for projects to be developed in the Barra da Tijuca neighborhood, a planned expansion area of the city. The 23 requests in the later period included 11 for changes of land use, 10 for building height, and the remaining two for occupation ratios or other changes. The operations generated US$26.7 million, with US$12 million in the peak year of 1999 (Xavier 2011).

The main criticisms of this approach involved issues of irregular management of the approvals, because many of them were not submitted to the Municipal Council of Urban Policy as required by the law. Underestimation of the value of additional building rights and the diversion of the funds from the original purpose were just two of the other abuses observed.

The possibility of paying the assessed valorization in special areas, such as historical heritage or environmental preservation projects, opened the way for underpayment of the effective accrued land value increment. Urban planners and other analysts also questioned its role in gentrifying the original neighborhoods, since most new social housing was built on the urban periphery.

These issues and other administrative irregularities created a social image of arbitrary decisions associated with political influence and corruption. The selling of zoning exceptions under criteria defined at a commission level rather than by a legislative body was deemed unconstitutional, and these operations were halted in 1998 in São Paulo and in 2000 in Rio de Janeiro (Cymbalista and Santoro 2006).

Participación en Plusvalías in Colombia

The 1997 Law 388 in Colombia addresses charges for changes in building rights through the *Participación en Plusvalías* instrument, whereby 30 to 50 percent of the assessed increased land values resulting from administrative actions, such as for density, zoning, or rural to urban land conversion, may also be subject to partial recovery by the public. Payments to be made in cash or in-kind are designated primarily for the provision of social housing and infrastructure in underserved neighborhoods, as well as for public works of general interest.

Despite initially high expectations for its success, the instrument has yet to show its strength. In Bogotá, revenues increased from about US$6 million in 2005 to US$8.5 million in 2008, US$25 million in 2011, and an expected US$40 million in 2012, but these amounts are considered far below the potential annual revenue (Parodi 2010).

Notwithstanding its conceptual consistency, the instrument's regulations are loaded with costly, cumbersome, and contradictory administrative procedures leading to conflicts and ample margin for different interpretations (Maldonado 2008). Elaborate guarantees to protect citizen interests created uncertainty for both public and private agents. The crux of the matter is the norm used to calculate the value of the increment, since it considers the situation before Law 388 was implemented and not the current situation.

From a legal perspective this opened the way for the recognition of acquired rights by landowners, reinforced by the fact that before the enactment of the law in 1997 many cities had overly generous, and often unlimited, norms and regulations regarding urban development projects. In addition, the implementation process and the administrative operation of the mandates are time-consuming and complex.

THE USE OF OODC IN BRAZIL

The instrument that regulates charges for additional building rights in Brazil (*Outorga Onerosa do Direito de Construir*, OODC) is based on the notion that the landowner's property right is limited to a basic FAR coefficient that is different from the maximum the area

could support. It imposes a charge for the right to develop land above a basic FAR as defined by the municipality up to a higher level established in its master plan. It also applies to other types of changes yielding more profitable land use options, such as conversions from rural to urban uses or the rezoning of areas for renovation or commercial uses.

The legitimacy of the charge is grounded in two ideas: the implicit understanding that in order to support the additional building rights or higher land uses the public has to provide investments in urban infrastructure and services; and second, the principle that the public cannot favor one property over others when granting additional building rights or new land uses. Thus, the instrument potentially allows all landowners to share the benefits resulting from public interventions supporting urban development.

A basic FAR is not necessarily set at 1, it may not be uniform across the city, and the percentage of the accrued land value increment also may vary. The city of Curitiba, for instance, has been selling building rights since 1991. Higher FARs were granted for free in some sectors of the city as an instrument to promote transit-oriented development in corridors where bus rapid transit systems where installed. The maximum FAR limit was raised even further for developers paying into a fund earmarked for social housing. The rights for building additional density were generally sold at less than the full appreciation value under the debatable premise that this policy would stimulate denser development, and thus help to defray part of the transit investment costs (Teixeira and Moreira 2011).

Calculating the Value of Building Rights

Different methods or formulas are used to calculate the land value increment resulting from the OODC, but all such methods have

© ALVARO URIBE

Charges for building rights in Curitiba, Brazil, have helped to promote transit-oriented development.

limited accuracy, since no two plots of land or development projects are perfectly comparable. In theory, the value of land developed with an FAR of 3 compared to a baseline FAR equal to 1 should be the difference between the residual values of their respective highest and best uses. In practice, this is not so simple since no two buildings in the area are the same and changes in some plots affect the highest and best use for nearby plots. Higher density is not always more profitable for developers, thus in certain areas the maximum allowable FAR may not be of interest to them, including in some high-end areas (Furtado and Silva 2010).

These complications are only partially resolved by the prevailing so-called virtual land method. Under this method a developer interested in a 750 m² building in a zone where the basic FAR is 1 and the maximum is equal to 3 could either acquire a plot of 750 m² or one of 250 m² and in addition acquire building rights through OODC to

build the additional 500 m² on the same plot. For this additional area the developer would be paying the equivalent of two more plots of land with the original or pre-existing FAR of 1 in the same area that has now been zoned for a higher FAR. This base square-meter value of land for the zone is obtained from the city valuation maps used for property taxation purposes. This method is used by cities such as Blumenau, Curitiba, Porto Alegre, Salvador, and São Luis (Furtado et al. 2010). Again, this is a proxy for the real value as conditions will change once an area is rezoned, but it allows for some consistency.

In practice, charges for additional building rights vary among jurisdictions applying the instrument, and difficulties in assessing the value of the additional building rights have led many jurisdictions to adopt shortcuts relying on base values that are proxies for or are only indirectly related to the accrued land value increment. The cities of Florianopolis and Natal, for example, calculate the charge as a percentage of the basic unit of construction cost applied to the additional area to be built, which some argue is more like a building permit fee (Furtado et al. 2010).

Adjustment factors to the assessed value are also typical, with some of them defined not on technical but on politically negotiated grounds (e.g., in the municipalities of Goiânia and Alvorada). While Campo Grande charges a fixed 70 percent of the estimated land value increment, Salvador simply applies 50 percent over the original value on the property. Though some cities refer to the estimated market value, others rely on the fiscal value (Furtado et al. 2010).

Challenges in the Application of OODC

The 2001 Statute of the City imposed a mandate on all municipalities to charge for any conceded building rights over and above the baseline. Many jurisdictions are still unwilling or unprepared to apply this legal mandate, and they circumvent it by setting the basic FAR coefficient at the maximum level. Since property rights are usually defined by national constitutional law, some analysts have concluded that to make OODC operative and consistent, the basic FAR should also be set at the national level, or an extra-municipal law should be enforced to reduce the vulnerability of local authorities to succumb to landowner interests.

An extreme case is Rio de Janeiro, whose administration has ignored the mandate, in part due to the city's ease in obtaining funds to prepare for the 2014 World Cup and 2016 Olympics. Its 1992 master plan established a basic FAR of 1 for the whole city, with higher maximum FARs in certain zones, although no initiatives have been taken to actually regulate charges for the corresponding building rights (Furtado and

Silva 2010). New master plan legislation in 2011 raised the basic FARs to 3 or 4 in places such as Copacabana and other high-end areas, with the possibility of designating even more areas under special circumstances, virtually eliminating the baseline for the charge.

The majority of Brazilian cities are not yet able to ensure implementation of this law. Challenges include the necessary existence of a master plan and zoning prescriptions, a detailed formula of how the building rights are to be assessed, forms of payment, definition of rules to apply the resources (usually by the establishment of a special fund), and a council to oversee the resources.

These requirements are out of reach for more than 90 percent of Brazil's 5,565 municipalities, especially those with a population below 50,000. According to the 2008 Municipal Management Survey (MUNIC) dedicated to land use norms and regulations, only 881 municipalities contemplated incorporating the OODC (let alone implementing it). Among the 1,626 municipalities with more than 20,000 inhabitants, 323 (about 20 percent) did not even have a master plan, in open violation of the 2001 statute (IBGE 2008).

On the other hand, promising progress has been made. In 2001 only 221 municipalities had passed the required legislation, whereas by 2009 the number increased to 1,059. In a study revisiting the 2005 MUNIC survey, a random sample of 60 municipalities out of the 241 municipalities with more than 50,000 inhabitants at the time stated they had the legislation for OODC, but in only 39 or 65 percent of them did it actually exist, and in only eight of those (or 13.3 percent of the full sample) was it being implemented effectively by 2007 (Cymbalista and Pollini 2009).

Consistent with other findings, the more qualitative study by Furtado et al. (2010)

found that many cities stating they had applied the OODC had actually relied on round-about formulas or other adjustment factors to accommodate local stakeholder interests (e.g., real estate developers and landowners), resulting in revenues at only symbolic levels.

In Curitiba, for example, in spite of the OODC's longstanding presence, the average annual revenue from 2007 to 2009 was about US$1.5 million (Teixeira and Moreira 2011). These values contrast dramatically with the performance of São Paulo, which earned more than US$50 million per year in that period, although they are quite different types of cities and Curitiba's population is only about one-third that of São Paulo (Sandroni 2010). In 2011 and 2012, Curitiba collected about US$17.5 million in ad hoc charges for building rights (*Gazeta do Povo* 2013) and São Paulo about US$250 million (Maleronka and Furtado 2013).

Implementation of OODC in São Paulo and Rio de Janeiro

To implement OODC in the municipality of São Paulo between 2002 and 2004, pre-existing FAR coefficients were reduced to 1, but in some areas an allowance was made to 1.5 and even 2. The city also redesigned the maximum FAR maps ranging from 1 to 4 (and thus the associated potential margins for applying the OODC). In some areas the FAR could then be lower than, equal to, or even higher than the original pre-existing FARs (table 4.1).

TABLE 4.1
Changes in FAR Coefficients in São Paulo, 2002–2004

Land Use Zones Established by the Strategic Development Plan in 2002	Land Use Zones before 2002	FAR up to 2002	Basic FAR		Maximum FAR
			In 2003	From 2004 on	
Exclusive Residential Zones (ZER)	Strict horizontal single-family residential zone (Z1)	1.0	1.0	1.0	1.0
Mixed Use Zones (ZM)	Predominant horizontal residences zone (Z9)	1.0	1.0	1.0	1.0
	Predominant low demographic density residential zone (Z2)	1.0	1.0	1.0	2.5
	Predominant low demographic density residential zone (Z11, Z13, Z17, Z18)	1.0	1.0	1.0	2.0
	Predominant medium demographic density residential zone (Z3, Z10, Z12)	2.5	2.0	2.0	4.0
	Mixed use zones and medium high demographic density zone (Z4)	3.0	2.5	2.0	4.0
	Mixed use zones and high demographic density zone (Z5)	3.5	3.0	2.0	4.0
	Special use zones (Z8 007-02, -04, -05, -08, -11, -12)	3.0	2.5	2.0	4.0
	Special use zones (Z8 007-10, -13)	2.0	2.0	2.0	4.0
	Special uses zones (Z8 060-01, -03)	1.5	1.0	1.0	2.5
	Mixed use with predominance of commerce and services zone (Z19)	2.5	1.5	1.0	4.0
Industrial Zones under Restructuring (ZIR)	Predominant industrial zone (Z6)	1.5	1.0	1.0	2.5
	Strict industrial zone (Z7)	1.0	1.0	1.0	2.5

Source: Adapted by the author from São Paulo municipal data.

Contrary to expectations, no major judicial cases were filed for what many may consider to be a reduction of land property rights, illustrating that properties that had not yet applied for building licenses could not necessarily claim acquired rights based on the pre-existing FARs (box 4.1). Clearly, land building potential was reduced, since a

Land value increments are generated after the authorization for a new land use is granted (usually through the building license). Before this occurs, only general norms and regulations are in place, and they do not actually generate rights or the possibility of charging for the increments. In other words, the request for the building license generates the right to demand payment as a result of new anticipated development.

This limitation is not a taking, as often suggested. Technically a taking occurs when a change in the norms and regulations leaves a property with no possibility of economic use—for instance, when the pre-existing norm allowed for housing and the area is now to be used only for forest conservation, with no possibility of commercial exploitation.

Alternatively, a taking would occur when a change in norms and regulations affects only one landowner, constituting a taking without compensation. A change in norms and regulations that still allows for the land to be used, albeit charging for it, is not a taking. No legislative body recognizes a public obligation to compensate for an unfavorable change of norms and regulations or for the elimination of rights for unrealized and as yet unauthorized land uses.

Signs adorn a multifamily property in Rio de Janeiro with APAC protection. The owners are protesting that it cannot be demolished so they could build a larger structure.

The sign states: "Mr. Mayor (Rio de Janeiro) — This APAC (designated area of cultural/historical/environmental protection) devalued our properties. A private property is the fruit of a life struggle!" However, this zoning regulation did not devalue the property, but rather affected the potential value if the property were to be converted for a more intensive use with a higher FAR.

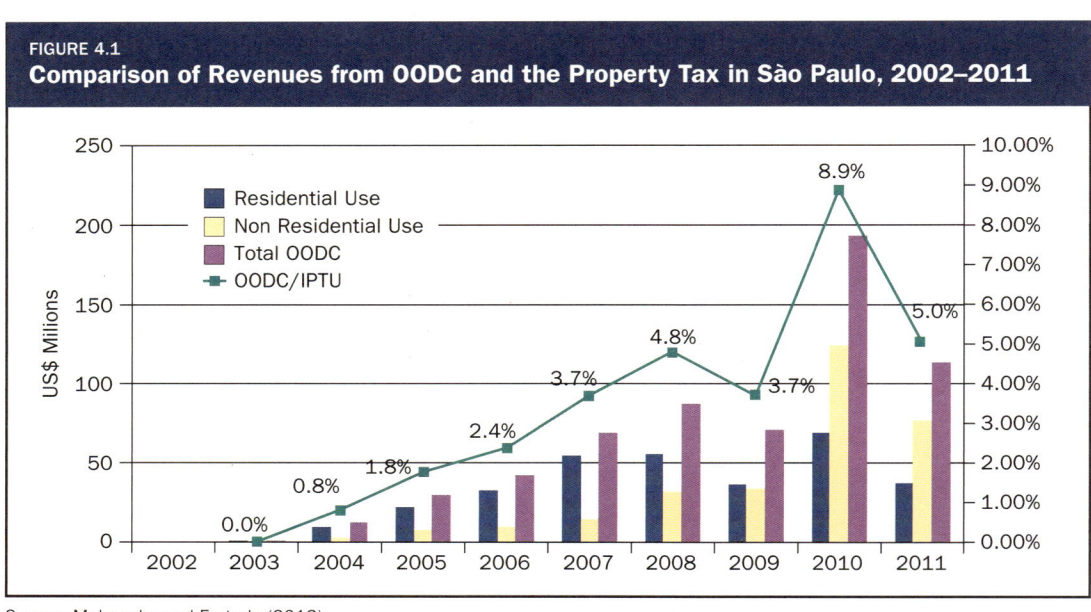

FIGURE 4.1

Comparison of Revenues from OODC and the Property Tax in São Paulo, 2002–2011

Legend:
- Residential Use
- Non Residential Use
- Total OODC
- OODC/IPTU

Source: Maleronka and Furtado (2013).

charge would now be imposed on what landowners previously perceived as a right to build free of any charges. Many factors may explain this outcome, the most important one being that at the time of implementation in 2004 the real estate market was expanding and thus veiled the net impact on landowners who viewed their property as combining land, buildings, and other improvements (Sandroni 2011). The success of the São Paulo case relative to Rio de Janeiro suggests that proper care in timing may be critical for changing the regulatory regime into one that can take advantage of value capture.

Figure 4.1 presents the revenues obtained from OODC payments over nine years that included the global financial crisis and its consequent restricted credit. These funds are deposited into the Urban Development Fund (FUNDURB), created to implement special plans and projects in urban and environmental areas or other interventions contemplated in São Paulo's 2002 municipal plan. In 2012 about US$175 million originating from OODC payments were

distributed through the FUNDURB by six municipal secretaries for projects including bus terminals, transportation corridors, parks and green areas, slum regularization, historical preservation, and drainage (Maleronka and Furtado 2013). With the increasing use of the instrument, future improvements expected as part of the mandate must take into account the realities of the real estate market.

TRANSFER OF DEVELOPMENT RIGHTS

Transfer of development rights (TDR) is a certificate by which the city administration compensates an owner in-kind for constraints on building rights imposed on the property (e.g., historical preservation or environmental conservation) or when the owner surrenders some of his land for a public interest project such as widening a road, creating a park, or rehabilitating a slum. These rights can be sold to third parties or used directly in developments in predefined receiving areas. The instrument has also been used to facilitate the imposition of stricter norms on building rights within certain areas, as when constraints are specific for FARs on single plots but not in the whole zone or sector where the plot is located. These principles are incorporated in urban legislation such as the Brazilian Statute of the City and Law 388 in Colombia.

In a successful TDR case, the municipality of Porto Alegre, Brazil, managed to acquire an extensive area for a new artery, 3a Avenida Perimetral, by compensating property owners with development rights that could be used elsewhere in the city. As a result of the 13.2 hectares of land acquired along the 12.3 km extension and 40-meter-wide avenue, including exclusive tracks for bus rapid transit, 50 percent of the cost (US$9.8 million) was covered by TDRs, representing 65 percent of the land acquired in a way that avoided expropriation or contested judicial orders (Uzon 2007).

The feasibility of this scheme was grounded in the city's policy since 1979, when the municipality began charging for development rights generated by land expropriated for public works such as parks and streets. Since the original building rights were already defined, development rights could be bought for use on other plots within the planning zone of the expropriated area or elsewhere in the city.

The absence of similar municipal prerogatives in the application of TDR in Mexico City is demonstrated in an attempt to use it in the late 1980s as a tool to finance the recovery of the historical center. Since no clear norms existed to impose on developers a charge for the additional building rights in the receiving area, the project relied on the discretionary concession of such rights by planning authorities. It was suspended in the 2000s under mounting

New transportation infrastructure in Porto Alegre, Brazil, is made possible by the use of transfer of development rights.

© CRISTINE ROCHOL / PORTO ALEGRE MUNICIPAL GOVERNMENT

suspicions of bribes for such concessions, as well as for lack of enforcement when certain landowners and investors requested more flexible land use norms and regulations, which were given generously, thus voiding the effectiveness of the TDR charges.

In another interesting application of TDR, the city of Curitiba raised the funds, originally estimated at US$45 million and later increased to US$62 million, for needed renovations of the Joaquim Américo soccer stadium, owned by the Atletico Paranaense Club, to comply with the rules of the International Federation of Football Associations for its use in the 2014 World Cup matches. To rebuild the stadium, Paraná's state government received a loan from the Brazilian National Development Bank (BNDES) to be transferred to the club, which in turn received building rights from the city to be used as collateral. Critics of this financial scheme argued that the large number of building rights being issued by the city would devalue the land and jeopardize the whole operation.

Care must be taken in applying TDRs and other instruments that charge for building rights such as the OODC. On the one hand a property owner may be properly compensated for building rights that must be surrendered, for example, for historical preservation purposes, but on the other hand developers must buy building rights if they want to build over and above the baseline. This can create confusion about how to compensate the owners whose building rights are taken.

A partial solution to this conundrum is to limit TDR compensation to the value of the actual building right up to the relevant baseline. Thus, if an historic building actually uses a FAR of .75 but the baseline FAR for the zone is 1.25 and the maximum FAR is 3.25, then the property owner may be compensated up to .50 (1.25-.75), not 2.5 (3.25-.75). Other developers would have to acquire the additional 2.0 FAR (3.25-1.25), but it would not be fair to compensate the historic property for that full amount.

CHAPTER 5
Value Capture Tools for Large Urban Redevelopment Projects

© ALVARO URIBE

Many cities in Latin America have initiated large-scale redevelopment projects in newly incorporated yet nonurbanized peripheral areas or in abandoned or vacant sections of older neighborhoods (Lungo 2004). The projects typically involve rezoning and updating the urban infrastructure and services, often resulting in significant benefits for the original landowners. Various instruments have been devised to defray some of the costs incurred. These initiatives have antecedents in the past, when entire neighborhoods were created by public utilities that used the land value increment on their serviced land to recover their own investments.

Urban reforms, like those initiated in Paris by Baron Haussmann, were also introduced in Latin America in the early twentieth century by Mayor Pereira Passos in Rio de Janeiro from 1903 to 1906 and by international urbanists such as Alfred Agache in his 1930 master plan for Rio de Janeiro and Karl Brunner's 1930 plan for Santiago, Chile, as well as in New Towns schemes for Caracas, Venezuela, and São Paulo, Brazil (Almandoz 2004). These plans included language referring implicitly to the internalization of prospective externalities created

Puerto Madero in Buenos Aires, Argentina, was redeveloped on public land in the old port district to stimulate economic recovery in the metropolitan region.

Renovated warehouses along the harbor canal bring visitors to Puerto Madero.

from the proposed well-designed, multi-faceted projects.

PRIVATIZING PUBLIC LAND FOR REDEVELOPMENT: PUERTO MADERO, BUENOS AIRES

The emblematic case of Puerto Madero in Buenos Aires comprised the urban renewal of 160 hectares of the old port located near downtown and owned by a federal agency, the General Administration of Ports (AGP). The redevelopment project was proposed in 1989 in the context of a financial crisis to promote economic recovery and job creation, as well as to reaffirm the primacy of downtown Buenos Aires within its metropolitan system.

A corporation was created to undertake the project with participation from the national and city governments. Over the last 20 years about 1.5 million m² of floor space has been developed, which is comparable to the annual rate of 1.5 to 3 million m² throughout the city of Buenos Aires. The state contributed the idle port land,

and more than US$2.26 billion in private investments have been triggered by the initiative. By 2011 the corporation had sold around US$230 million worth of land—a value resulting from the internalization of externalities created by the project. The proceeds funded public works worth US$113 million and an overhead for management fees and the like.

The initial investment included the land (assessed originally at US$60 million) and a set of intangible services (project design, expertise, consulting), reaching a total of US$120 million. Land values per square meter were originally set at US$150–300, were later traded at US$600, and today exceed US$1,000. Most of the recent valorization is no longer captured by the corporation but by private investors who reap the benefits from their control of large parts of the development area.

The project has contributed four major waterways covering 39 hectares and 28 hectares of green space for the city's park system. Puerto Madero today is a premier tourist destination of Buenos Aires and has stimulated development in the central city as intended. In 2011 the corporation transferred the maintenance of all areas to the city government, but retains the concessions on water bodies, piers, and parking lots as a source of income; it also kept two properties with an estimated sale value of about US$30 million. All in all, the project is considered to be a creative innovation in urban management in terms of self-financing mechanisms and interjurisdictional cooperation in urban governance (Garay 2012).

Critics of the project argue that it represented a give-away of a public asset to private interests, resulting in one of the most gentrified neighborhoods in an exclusive area detached from the urban fabric. Questions have been raised about the lack of public participation in the decision-making process, which could have brought to the agenda other, more socially responsible uses for the area, especially in the context of the economic crisis when many urgent priorities needed to be addressed.

PUBLIC ACQUISITION OF PRIVATE LAND: NUEVO USME, BOGOTÁ

Other initiatives throughout the region are designed to share in the resulting land value increment and/or defray part of the public investment costs needed to rezone and restructure large tracts of the urban fabric. These efforts involve original or prospective landowners in exchange for their receiving a share of future revenues. More challenging and rare are cases where a value capture strategy is used to self-finance the provision of serviced land to meet the needs of low-income families. The cases of the Social Urbanizer experiment in Porto Alegre, Brazil (Smolka and Damasio 2005; Damasio 2006) and the Nuevo Usme project, though still unfinished, are emblematic for their boldness and combination of value capture tools.

Usme is an area located in the southeastern sector of Bogotá, where some 900 hectares have already been developed by powerful pirate (illegal) subdividers who provide no services or infrastructure and do not have proper approvals from the public administration. In June 2000 the city's master plan allocated another 800 hectares for urban expansion and set up *Operación Urbanística Nuevo Usme* (OUNU), a project designed to address the problem of illegal developments. It is expected to expand into another 600 hectares where the administration already has invested in water and sewer systems, extension of the bus rapid transit system, and construction of low-income housing units (Maldonado and Smolka 2003).

OUNU involves the planning and management of 432 hectares for collective uses, such as roads, protected areas, open space and recreation areas, and other amenities, and 368 hectares for 56,000 housing units. Over 40 percent of these units will be on developed plots that will also include housing for higher-income families, and 67.5 hectares of land will be allocated for commercial and agro-industrial uses. The OUNU project was originally conceived to provide a competitive and sustainable alternative to the informal yet affordable land offered by pirate subdividers.

The core idea for this project was to mobilize the land value increment in low-income urbanization processes. In such cases, raw land is typically traded at less than US$3/m²; the cost of fully servicing land ranges from US$10 to US$35/m²; and the fully serviced land provided by the formal market is conservatively estimated at more than US$55/m². In contrast, unserviced land sold by pirate subdividers is generally about US$28/m². The self-financing OUNU scheme would rely on three key value capture tools: acquisition of land at prices set before the announcement of the project;

© MARTIM O. SMOLKA

The Nuevo Usme development project in Bogotá, Colombia, was designed to provide affordable housing and other services by using various value capture tools.

a partial plan to readjust the land of those landowners that agree to dispose of their land for the project instead of having it expropriated; and the use of *Participatión in Plusvalías* as a tool to share the land value increment resulting from the changes of land uses.

The plan was to offer local landowners the option to either be expropriated at the prevailing assessed land price before 2000, or to entrust their land to the project with a guaranteed return on the sale of the land in proportion to their contribution, the number of participants, and the overall land appreciation, net of all urbanization costs and the share designated for the public benefit.

To ensure affordability by the new lower-income inhabitants, a cross-subsidy scheme ranged from an affordable $16/m² for serviced housing lots up to $80/m² for commercial lots, $21/m² for serviced lots combining housing and commerce on the main roads, and up to $70/m² for housing lots for higher-income families. Although about two-thirds of the land was acquired though public expropriations, the remaining one-third was obtained through voluntary

negotiations with landowners who accepted the sharing of costs and benefits entailed in the corresponding partial plan.

Given the project's magnitude, extended timetable, and innovative character, its implementation has not been continuous or smooth. Over the last decade it has been interrupted many times by other administrative and political priorities, changing institutional organizations, and unanticipated obstacles. Three new challenges are now being addressed: the designation of a significant part of the area as a National Forest Reservation; the discovery of an archaeological site; and a movement by local peasants, supported by the current administration, against a densification policy for the region.

These interruptions and periods of public inaction have allowed opportunistic pirate subdividers to sell land at a premium in the expectation of future regularization and increasing land values. While the original idea of self-financing the provision of serviced land to low-income families with the land value increment generated by the project still holds, more ad hoc decisions have been taken independently for different zones of the project, compromising some aspects of the overall plan.

LAND READJUSTMENT

In complex cases where parcels in a project area belong to many individuals, coordinating their interests to generate a win-win result is difficult. It often requires the establishment of a third-party public, semi-public, or even private entity in the form of a trust with a mandate to carry out the development.

One such instrument to promote the development of large areas is land readjustment. As implied by its name, its value capture logic is based on in-kind (usually land) contributions by all landowners in the area to an entity that in turn uses (sells) these contributions to self-finance investment in urban infrastructure and services that then increases the value of all properties in the area (figure 5.1). Although the plots of each original landowner are readjusted into a

different size and shape, the overall value of each plot should be higher due to the investments. That is, the participants expect that the appreciation resulting from urbanization will more than compensate for the smaller size of each readjusted plot, and they bear that risk.

The concept of land readjustment dates to the nineteenth century in Germany and has been used extensively in Asia (Japan and Korea) and many European countries. The Spanish version has influenced the redevelopment schemes of Colombian partial plans, and the French *zone d'aménagement concerté* (urban development zone) has influenced the Brazilian program known as urban operations.

Partial Plans in Colombia
An antecedent for the application of land readjustment in Colombia can be found in Law 9 of 1989, which included a provision for land assembly through direct acquisition

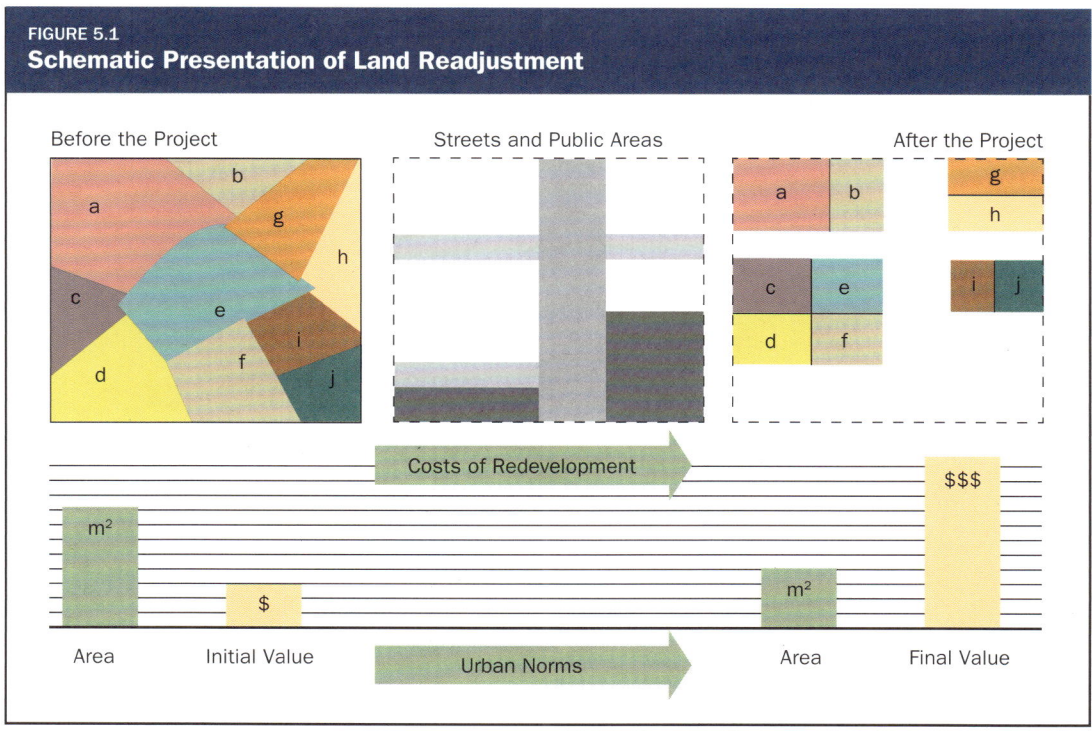

FIGURE 5.1
Schematic Presentation of Land Readjustment

Before the Project   Streets and Public Areas   After the Project

Costs of Redevelopment

Area   Initial Value   Urban Norms   Area   Final Value

Source: Created by Maria Cristina Rojas Eberhard (2011).

or expropriation, and allowed readjustment of plots after urban infrastructure and services were implemented. The urbanization agency Metrovivienda, for instance, buys and urbanizes land and then contracts or sells the land to private builders of social housing as a tool to keep final prices affordable. Law 388 of 1997 later introduced a mandate for land readjustment to either obtain a better overall configuration of the individual properties or to ensure a just redistribution of benefits and costs.

Landowners holding a minimum of 51 percent of the area can submit a proposed land use plan if it meets the parameters of a partial plan—an intermediate planning instrument between a full areawide master plan and a smaller neighborhood or block plan. It adjusts broad city guidelines to lower-scale conditions and relies on various value capture tools, including land readjustment and betterment contributions (Rojas Eberhard and Rave 2013). The project is managed by a specially created independent entity, and reluctant owners are either required to sell or are subject to administrative expropriation. Although cities like Bogotá and Medellín have initiated many partial plans, cases of fully embedding land readjustment principles are less common. Some places include a redefinition of land use configuration, if not by shape of the original plots then by the assignment of different densities.

The Simesa project in Medellín illustrates the redevelopment of the site of a former steel mill and other smaller factories into a fully self-funded, high-end residential complex (figure 5.2). In the area of about 30 hectares, one original industry still owns

FIGURE 5.2
Proposed Land Readjustment Plan for Simesa Project in Medellín, Colombia

Source: Rojas Eberhard and Rave (2013).

An aerial view of the Simesa project in Medellín, Colombia, shows the site under construction in 2011. One of the former steel mills on the site in 2006 has been demolished as part of the redevelopment.

© VALORES SIMESA

© VALORES SIMESA

46 percent of the land, three other companies own another 49 percent, and 18 businesses own the remaining 5 percent, each with a plot of less than 1,250 m². The area was readjusted to accommodate 37 units on 13 plots and set aside 37 percent of the land for parks, green zones, and streets. In the remaining area, an occupation rate of 80 percent was imposed on each plot to be used for residential and commercial uses.

The full amount of the urbanization costs for the area corresponded to about 23 percent of the total value, and it was fully funded or recovered from the building sales revenues at the same time that land value increased about 19 percent (Rojas Eberhard and Rave 2013). This is a particularly interesting case since a phased-in timeframe was negotiated for the relocation of the departing factories simultaneously with the redesign of the area to accommodate new residential and commercial uses. The public administration thus played an important role by enforcing the fundamental urban design, land use norms, and land sharing schemes. It also ensured equitable adjustments among the participating landowners by informing them about the partial plans and the procedure for sharing costs and benefits.

In cases where a significant component of the land is devoted to social housing, buyers often cannot afford the full cost of the construction, let alone the urbanization costs. The land for public uses and social housing would then typically be acquired by a public entity at the price set prior to announcement of the project. These new uses may allow for some shared benefits, but normally do not cover all urbanization costs. However, the net costs of these interventions on the site are often less than if they were developed elsewhere.

An example is the Pajarito Partial Plan in the expansion zone of Medellín. It involves the assembly of 38 plots from 36 landowners in an area of 230 hectares. Nearly 87 percent of the plots are privately owned and 18 percent of them are already developed. Thirty percent of the area will be occupied and 36 percent will be protected for environmental purposes. Thus, of the original 230 hectares, only 6.3 hectares remain for residential and other new uses, once the pre-designated areas are netted out. The project is designed to provide social housing in high-density, eight-story buildings holding 100 to 238 housing units. The urban infrastructure and services costs amounted to about US$45 million. The municipality acquired 80 percent of the land through voluntary sales at prices not incorporating future land value expectations and sold the final units at prices that recovered all urbanization costs (Rojas Eberhard and Rave 2013).

Although the principles behind using land readjustment to provide self-financed access to serviced land for the urban poor seem feasible, projects have not been easy to implement. This is apparently due to the stress imposed on the one hand by the need for subsidies to cover lower-income housing prices, and on the other by the reluctance of landowners to participate in projects designed to address low-income social policies. Attempts to rely on land readjustment principles in the reconstruction effort after the Chilean earthquake in 2010 exposed the distrust of private individual landowners toward cooperative market-oriented solutions (Hong and Brain 2012).

Urban Operations in Brazil

An urban operation (*Operación Urbanística*, UO) is defined by the Brazilian Statute of the City as a tool to promote the restructuring of large areas of the city through land-based incentives offered to public-private partnerships including local public authorities, developers, landowners, and other stakeholders as independent investors (Montandon and de Souza 2007). In practical terms, it is a significant intervention that requires infrastructure and urban improvements, such as avenues, drainage, public spaces and facilities, and other investments. The fund-

ing should come from the incremental value stimulated by the public investments, zoning, and other land use changes (Sandroni 2010).

In its original formulation the public would retain a certain percentage (usually around 50 percent) of the land value increment (Sandroni 2010). Unlike in linkage operations, the value that is captured is reverted into the defined area in the form of investments in social housing and related infrastructure and services. Each of the urban operations currently underway in the city of São Paulo has its own footprint design, objective, and strategy, and relies on different formulas and parameters to self-finance its implementation (figure 5.3).

Other Examples

Other types of public-private development projects focus on the redevelopment of degraded, deteriorated, abandoned, or simply vacant areas owned by diverse owners who are invited or brought together (by voluntary or mandatory means) to agree on the terms for an urban regeneration project in which they may or may not participate in the conception, design, and execution. The terms may include "readjusting" their respective parcels of land, some sharing of the project proceeds, and direct apportioning of the necessary investment capital for the enterprise.

Examples include the Eixo Tamanduathey redevelopment of a deactivated industrial area on over 900 hectares in the municipality of Santo André in the São Paulo metropolitan area (Figueiredo 2005); and the Santa Fe redevelopment of a former sand mine into a new business center next to a park built on a converted garbage dump in Mexico City. In the Mexico case, a public trust, SERVIMET (*Servicios Metropolitanos del Gobierno del Distrito Federal*), was established in the late 1990s and the plan was defined in 1997 to dispose of the public land in ways that would fund the urban infrastructure and services. The project was discontinued in 2003 following public disclosures of political influence and misconduct. Rents per square meter are now about US$20, similar to the city's high-valued Lomas de Chapultepec area, but the redevelopment is imposing significant costs on the city to address the traffic congestion it generated.

AUCTIONING ADDITIONAL BUILDING RIGHTS: CEPACS IN BRAZIL

Given the difficulties in valuing a change in building rights, an ingenious solution relies on what developers are actually willing to pay (or bid) under competitive market conditions. The city of São Paulo first introduced Certificates of Additional Potential Construction Bonds (CEPACs) in 1995 to simulate the bidding process through which urban land prices are ultimately determined.

The main idea is that the new development potential, such as for different types of uses and additional buildings, created by rezoning and public investments in a well-defined area should not be available for free, as in the past, but auctioned among those interested in taking advantage of the future economic benefits resulting from the public interventions.

The municipality issues the CEPAC bonds corresponding to these building rights for purchase by competing developers through public electronic auctions regulated by the *Comissão de Valores Mobiliários* (CVM, the Brazilian equivalent of the U.S. Securities and Exchange Commission). CVM registers the urban operation to which the CEPACs are linked in the master plan, authorizes the auctions, and monitors any initiative to change the plan. The mechanism has become the most original and effective instrument to mobilize land value increment generated by large-scale urban projects.

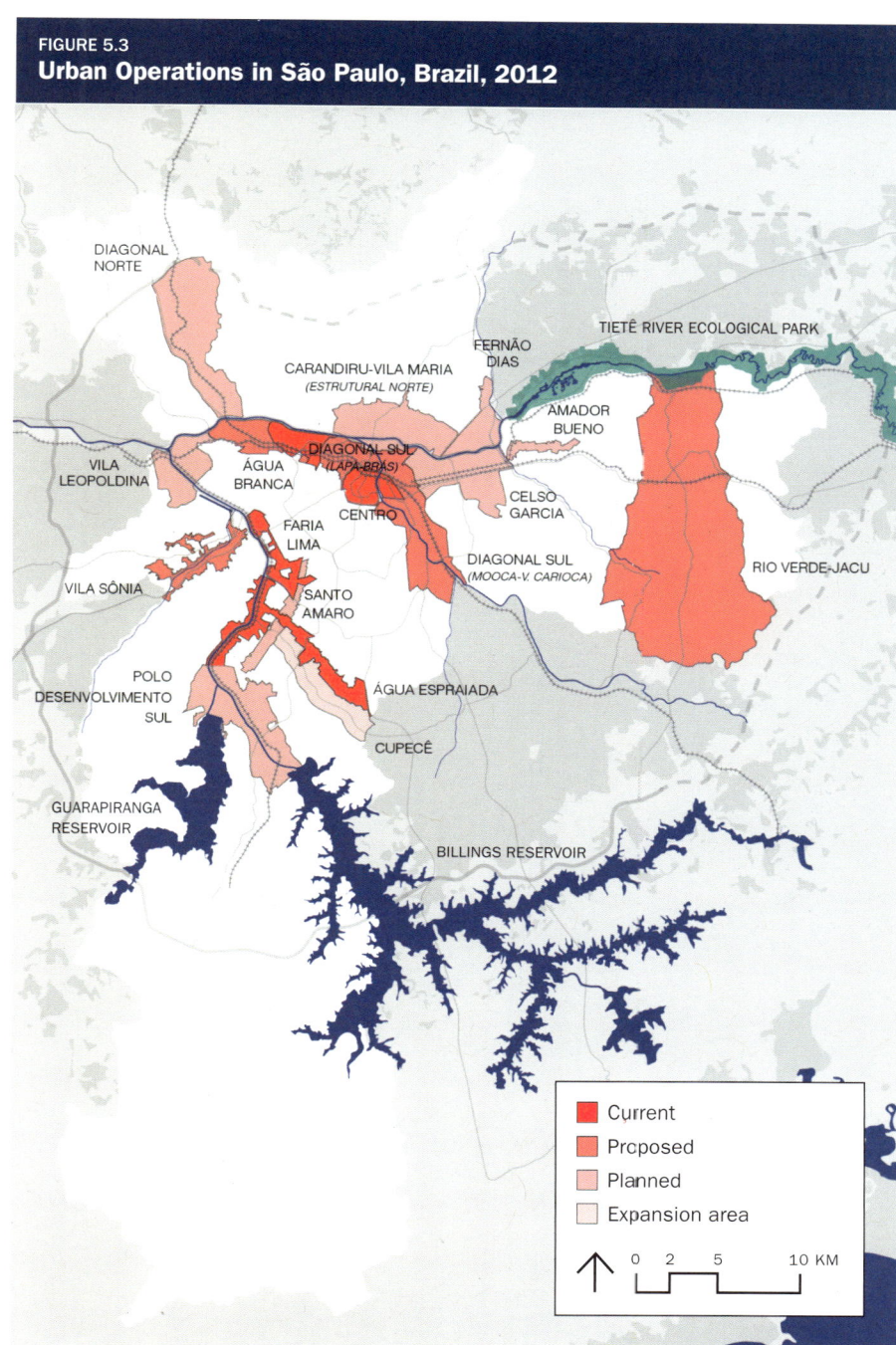

FIGURE 5.3
Urban Operations in São Paulo, Brazil, 2012

Source: Municipal Secretariat for Urban Development, São Paulo.

Selling CEPACs at public auction on the stock exchange resolves the problem that previously inhibited the sale of development rights by providing a regulated, transparent, and reasonable way to determine their value (Sandroni 2010). The financial regulations also require significant transparency in a public auction, and all relevant documents are available on the Internet. São Paulo's stock exchange website lists CEPACs as one of the financial instruments traded along with stocks and mutual funds.

The license to build over and above the basic FAR within the defined area requires payment in CEPACs based on the number of additional square meters the developer applies for. Usually one CEPAC is needed for each square meter of building rights, but since neighborhoods or zones within the site may differ in quality, adjustments are made within a range from 2 to 0.5 m^2 for more or less desirable locations. The urban operation generally involves rezoning and associated urban infrastructure updating that in turn supports a given volume of buildings according to the plan. The prefixed number of building rights may be auctioned in small offerings over time or in a single sale.

The city of São Paulo has been offering periodic auctions as a market control strategy to enhance the value of the bids. In the seven auctions held for the Faria Lima UO from 2004 to 2010, the winning bids raised between US$550 and US$2,000 per CEPAC for 682,669 offered and 638,074 actually bought, raising a total of US$723 million (table 5.1). Since a vigorous demand-driven market existed for the area, with some bids being negotiated up to US$3,500 per CEPAC, the mayor requested the City Council to release an additional 350,000 m^2 in the area to be covered by 500,000 CEPACs. The recently elected mayor subsequently froze the request, arguing that the area was already too congested.

Five auctions for the Agua Espraiada UO from 2004 to 2012 raised from US$172 to US$636 per CEPAC for more than 3 million offered, generating nearly US$1.5 billion (table 5.2). The 2012 auction alone added US$866 million to public coffers, on top of results from previous auctions (Sandroni 2013). More than one public auction may take place between the dates of authorized CVM distributions; thus, the figures for

TABLE 5.1
Public and Private Auctions of CEPACs in Faria Lima UO, São Paulo, 2004–2010

Year and Type	# CEPACs Offered	# CEPACs Sold	Price (US$)	Income (US$)
2004				
Public	90,000	9,091	550	5,000,050
Private	na	24,991	550	13,745,050
2005				
Public	0			
Private	na	9,778	550	5,377,900
2006				
Public	10,000	2,729	550	1,500,950
Private	na	6,241	550	3,432,550
2007				
Public	156,730	156,730	620	97,172,600
Private	na	72,942	620	45,224,040
2008				
Public	83,788	83,788	769	64,432,972
Private	na	2,500	863	2,156,250
2009				
Public	100,000	55,612	850	47,270,200
Public	30,000	1,521	858	1,304,258
Public	120,000	120,000	2,100	252,000,000
2010				
Public	92,151	92,151	2,000	184,302,000
Total	682,669	638,074		722,918,820

Notes: Private auctions are promoted occasionally by the city as an alternative form of payment to the contractors it hires for public works projects in urban operations. The number of CEPACs offered in private auctions is not available (na).

Source: Sandroni (2012).

US$ per CEPAC refer to the average value obtained in all auctions. In addition, a considerable number of CEPACs are still in circulation because they have not yet been used in a license application. As of January 31, 2013, the city still had nearly 360,000 CEPACs available to offer in auctions.

Although the most successful and longest standing cases are found in São Paulo, other Brazilian cities have issued CEPACs. For instance, all the building rights issued for the Porto Maravilha revitalization project in Rio de Janeiro's old port area were bid by a single buyer, the Real Estate Development Fund created by Caixa Econômica Federal (CEF), the Brazilian social and housing bank with funds it manages from the workers' pension funds. Law 101 of November 23, 2009 had authorized issuing 6,436,722 CEPACs for a total of 4,089,502 m² of additional building rights

TABLE 5.2

CEPACs Authorized for the Agua Espraiada UO, São Paulo, through January 31, 2013

Authorized Distributions by CVM	CEPACs	US$	US$ per CEPAC (average)
14/7/2004	299,368	51,404,360	172
10/1/2007	317,781	65,304,996	206
23/12/2008	186,740	103,640,520	555
5/9/2008	1,099,880	386,461,945	351
9/2/2012	1,360,338	865,676,658	636
Total	3,263,907	1,447,488,659	443
Private Offers	127,092	25,664,266	202
Grand Total	3,390,999	1,473,152,925	434
Used for a License / Completed Projects	−2,333,897		
Remaining in Circulation	1,057,102		
Total CEPACs	3,750,000		
Balance	359,001		

Note: CVM is the Brazilian equivalent of the U.S. Securities and Exchange Commission.

Source: Municipality of São Paulo, Secretariat of Urban Development.

The bridge and other developments in the Agua Espraiada UO in São Paulo, Brazil, were funded by the auctioning of CEPACs.

© MARTIM O. SMOLKA

A new highway and parkland in the Linha Verde UO in Curitiba, Brazil, were partially funded by CEPACs.

for US$1.75 billion. The municipality of Rio de Janeiro thus obtained a substantial amount upfront to cover the costs of re-urbanizing that area.

Since CEPACs can be freely negotiated in a secondary market, CEF is expected to auction its supply of the bonds over time to other parties. In October 2012 alone, CEF sold about 26,000 CEPACs (out of 100,000 offered) at a base price of US$575, obtaining US$30 million in an operation that achieved a 100 percent gain over the original acquisition price per CEPAC.

CEPACs are also being used to partially fund the Linha Verde UO in Curitiba (Soffiatti 2012). This project involves the conversion of a major national highway, now engulfed by city expansion and cutting across 22 neighborhoods, into an urban avenue with the extension of a bus rapid transit line, new green areas, and higher-density land uses. For this $600 million

investment, a municipal decree in 2012 authorized the release of 4,830,000 CEPACs with a minimum initial price of US$100 per CEPAC. The first auction in the São Paulo stock market in June 2012 attracted 18 bidders for the 141,588 bonds offered. A group of three bidders associated with the development of a shopping center acquired 70 percent of the CEPACs.

Although Curitiba's mayor's office expected to collect US$30 million, the auction resulted in only US$14.2 million, since all the CEPACs traded at the minimum legal value of US$100 (*Gazeta do Povo* 2012). Though low, this price was close to what had been estimated for the market value by a private consultant hired to do the feasibility study on the use of CEPACs in this peripherally located project.

The CEPAC instrument offers both innovative characteristics and some negative aspects. On the positive side:

1. It addresses the difficult issue of assessing the market value of the increment resulting from the public interventions and reduces the traditional transaction costs involved in negotiating the relevant impacts of the project on individual properties.
2. It is accepted by developers who understand the benefit of having all revenues invested in the same area. By law the revenues from CEPAC auctions are kept in a separate account and can be used only in the same UO where they were generated.
3. It creates a self-fulfilling public investment opportunity: the higher the expectation of the benefits of the intervention, the higher the bids and consequently the revenues to insure its effective implementation (and vice versa). Thus, CEPACs actually draw strength from the speculative land process because higher bidding in the secondary market signals action in the primary market, thus increasing the amount of value captured.

On the other hand:
1. A relatively sophisticated capital market environment is required to support the credibility of the CEPAC bonds and the process for their access and disposal, thus limiting their use in less-developed areas.
2. Although there is nothing implicit in the tool that prevents its use in low-income areas and for social housing, the combination of lower payment capacity and perceived negative externalities may decrease bids below the threshold costs for public investment. The need to add a subsidy for low-income housing may introduce further complications into the auction process (Whitaker Ferreira 2012).
3. If the municipal development agency decides that social housing will lower demand and it wants to maximize overall auction prices, then it will be more likely to promote gentrification, resulting in more intra-urban differentiation and social segregation. A more realistic reaction to this allegation would argue that if these projects are implemented anyway they should be funded by the direct beneficiaries rather than all citizens or taxpayers.

The test for these pros and cons is whether the urban operation precedes the use of CEPACs or whether the opportunity to use this instrument negatively affects the nature of the subsequent development. Maricato and Ferreira (2002) argue that such value capture instruments are in themselves neutral so they can be used to create a more democratic and equitable city, or to do the opposite. How they are used, therefore, will depend in large part on the decisions of the elected representatives and appointed policy makers. Will they seek more social objectives or try to maximize auction prices?

CHAPTER 6
Conclusions and Recommendations

© MINISTRY OF THE CITIES, BRASILIA

Officials and other participants gather in Brasilia to launch Brazil's first Conference of the Cities in 2003.

Value capture policies and tools are undeniably arousing new interest and becoming more acceptable in Latin America. Initiatives to understand and experiment with the basic economic principles behind value capture have grown in both number and creativity, and value capture tools are being used in combination with traditional practices in many cases.

Public authorities are realizing that they can raise contributions for the public good from the beneficiaries of their administrative decisions. They can negotiate or charge for changes in land use rights or in the location and timing of public works directly with those private landowners or developers who seek access to urban services or want to develop new land uses beyond baseline norms and regulations. Changing the distribution of social costs and private benefits is also being addressed through new legislation, policy design, and implementation. Improved understanding of the link between public intervention and increased land value is conducive to building fiscal and planning cultures that will strengthen property taxes, local revenues, and urban management in general.

KEY FINDINGS AND LESSONS

The growing familiarity with and use of value capture in Latin America is supported by broader dissemination of longstanding practices in several countries and by the need to find new revenue sources to address current fiscal and urban planning challenges. National legislation, as in Brazil and Colombia, and a variety of municipal initiatives, as in Córdoba, Argentina, and Cuenca, Ecuador, have been designed to capture changes in land value increments resulting from public works and administrative actions. Rather than reinventing the wheel, many places are implementing changes that reflect the consolidation and systematization of established principles about value capture to meet local needs (table 6.1).

In many places urban development projects have produced financial windfalls

TABLE 6.1
Choosing the Appropriate Value Capture Tool

Tool	Incidence	Context	Process for Capturing Value	Advantages	Cautions	Pre-Existing Capacity
Public Land Procurement	ESC	Land needed for new public projects, such as low-income housing	Confiscation of changes in land value from prior use	Public investments made prior to development	Arbitrary decisions from unprepared courts	Legitimate public utilities to participate in the process
Property or Land Value Tax	EMC	Properties benefiting from citywide improvements	Rate imposed on land value component	Universality and regularity	Land vs. building component of property value	Continuous updating of value maps and cadastres
Exactions	NSV	Public concessions on new developments	In-kind or monetary compensation	Flexibility allowing for unanticipated developments	Manipulation or stakeholder influence	Access to information about private gains and public impacts
Betterment Contribution	EMC	Provision of local public works	Cost recovery or sharing	Beneficiaries invest in the project	Accurate assessment cf potential benefits	Capacity of beneficiaries to participate and pay
Transfer of Development Rights	ESC	Public interest in designated property	Compensation with rights given in other properties	Building rights used as currency to fund public projects	Accuracy of conversion rates for development rights	Availability of building rights in the transfer areas
Land Readjustment	NMV	Urbanization of a new area or reconfiguring of existing parcels	Sale of shares in the redeveloped land	Funding of new urban infrastructure	Obstructions from unwilling landowners	Power to negotiate with all affected participants
Charges to Building Rights	NSC	Single building license	Land assessment techniques	Compensation to the public for existing infrastructure	Allegations of acquired rights	Land monitoring and cadastral systems
CEPACs	NMC	New or redeveloped projects with broader urban impacts	Public auction	Transparency and accuracy in transactions and assessments	Market volatility; gentrification	Public credibility and capacity for financial management

Key to Incidence:
First letter: E–Improvement to existing land uses; N–Promotion of a new land use
Second letter: S–Single project or property; M–Multiple projects or properties
Third letter: V–Voluntary or negotiated; C–Compulsory

from public interventions that increased land values that formerly were appropriated by the benefitted landowners, but now are being shared with the public. Although the dollar value of these captured resources has often been small, the potential for growth is significant, as illustrated in the cases of Bogotá's betterment contributions or São Paulo's auctioning of building rights through CEPACs. More accurate indicators of success than the share of overall revenues may be either the magnitude of proceeds from value capture mechanisms compared to direct local investment costs for urban infrastructure, social housing, and other local services, or the role these proceeds play in promoting private investments by funding compensation for special projects, urban operations, partial plans, or other incentive programs.

The betterment instrument has been applied successfully, even in places with apparent technical or administrative constraints, to support a variety of local investments, especially those associated with transportation. According to García Bolivar (2012), director of the Valorization Fund (FONVAL) of Medellín, "More than 50 percent of Medellín's main road grid was paid for with betterment levies" (figure 6.1). In Mexico, although betterment contributions represented only .11 percent of public revenues, they covered 1.53 percent of all public works. In the municipality of Cuenca, Ecuador, nearly US$106 million collected as betterment contributions resulted in paving 270 km of roads. These examples counter the argument that the revenues from value capture policies may not be worth the effort.

Value capture instruments that charge for building rights have provided partial or full funding for major urban redevelopment projects in many cities. As a result, resources can be transferred from public infrastructure budgets for other social sectors (e.g., education, health, and housing) that in the past would have been sacrificed because of overall constraints on public expenditures.

Contrary to conventional wisdom or objections raised by opponents, the legal framework regarding value capture approaches in most countries is not particularly constraining. In many instances current legislation followed rather than preceded successful cases of value capture implementation, demonstrating that existing instruments can be adapted to new circumstances without having to wait for national legislation to be put in place first. Examples of this process include separating building rights from land rights and thus allowing for charges for building rights in Brazil; the adoption of the compensatory price mechanism in Montevideo, Uruguay, seven years ahead of national legislation; and increased acceptance by private investors of exactions in Guatemala and Argentina.

Effective implementation remains the primary challenge, according to the results obtained in two Lincoln Institute surveys of public officials and others involved with urban management and public finance in the region. The online questionnaires sought to elicit respondents' views about the prospects for designing, institutionalizing, and implementing two emblematic value capture instruments—betterment contributions and charges for additional building rights. The results revealed that value capture is still viewed primarily as a tool to promote equity in cities, rather than as a way to improve municipal fiscal autonomy and urban development in general (Smolka 2012).

Another result, confirmed by other research for this report, is that the impact of successful value capture policies on real estate development has been minimally disruptive, and that willingness to pay is directly associated with the perception of

FIGURE 6.1
Roadways Funded by Betterment Contributions in Medellín, Colombia, 1938–2000

Source: Mayor's Office of Medellín.

received benefits. This important finding applies both to charges for building rights for developers and to cost-sharing for individual taxpayers of public investments benefiting their affected properties.

Experience counts. The number and quality of value capture experiences in a country or municipality tend to be synergistic and cumulative. That is, success with one type of instrument leads to additional initiatives and the use of other instruments. It is not by chance that some countries, notably Brazil and Colombia, have been cited more often than others due to their experiences in using different applications and their many experiments with value capture tools. There is even some evidence of jurisdictions effectively changing the "rules of the game" for

property development and enlisting the support of developers who recognize that some value capture provisions were actually improving their business opportunities.

Changing from the prevailing complacency toward property development, whereby individual landowners capitalize unearned income from public investments, into a new regime, in which private benefits are balanced with social costs, involves a painstaking cultural shift that may take a long time and is expected to face significant resistance. Special care should be given to the appropriate and consistent use of value capture instruments and other elements in the planning toolbox.

Resistance to value capture policies and the use of related tools needs to be overcome in three ways: ideology, interests, and igno-rance. First, regarding *ideology*, ensure that the alleged additional public involvement in the market, as implied by basic value capture principles, can actually improve conditions for new business opportunities and for the community as a whole. Second, recognize that *interests* other than those of landowners have a legitimate stake in urban development. Third, counter *ignorance* with sound knowledge that charges on land values are not inflationary but in fact are capitalized in lower market prices; that rights are acquired only when a license is requested to promote a land use change; and that the rights of property do not necessarily include the right to the intrinsic land value or unearned increments in value.

Value capture: It should be done, it can be done, it has been done . . . and it may be done better.

RECOMMENDATIONS

These conclusions point to steps that can be taken in three spheres: learning from varied experiences with the implementation of value capture policies and tools; increas-ing knowledge about the complex nature of varied value capture approaches; and promoting greater understanding among public officials and citizens about how value capture tools can be used to benefit their communities.

Learn from Implementation Experiences

The city's built environment is the cumula-tive result of multiple land use decisions em-bodied in infrastructure and buildings that affect other uses over long periods of time. Planners and developers thus operate under high levels of uncertainty and risk when any charges or other types of regulations are proposed that may affect existing or new land uses. While value capture charges in theory are neutral regarding land use and should fall entirely on landowners, in prac-tice successful implementation demands management skills to deal with many com-plex factors and diverse stakeholders. In addition it requires proper understanding of land market conditions, comprehensive property monitoring systems, a fluid dia-logue among fiscal, planning, and judicial entities, and the political resolve of local government leaders. Key steps are to:

- Ensure the proper timing of any proposed change from a traditional regulatory regime into one contemplating value capture tools that are appropriate to existing real estate market conditions.

- Recognize that trial-and-error is part of the process of refining and institutional-izing any policy tool, including value capture, and that there is no one-size-fits-all solution.

- Prioritize the public control of building rights and land uses rather than focus on state ownership of land as elements of a value capture strategy.

- Maintain updated cadastres, valuation maps, and land and housing price records to generate the data needed to assess the impact and equitable sharing of changes in land values.

- Ensure administrative continuity in the implementation of value capture policies over time, especially for large-scale projects, to facilitate a less volatile environment that is more compatible with the matura-tion of long-term impacts.

- Encourage direct negotiations between public officials and the private developers who will benefit from specific public interventions.

- Generate a willingness to pay when the benefit is perceived to be associated directly with the solution of a locally recognized problem.
- Create a win-win situation resulting in significant land value increments being returned to a well-defined area as a result of public intervention.

Increase Knowledge about Theory and Practice

Conducting research, documenting and disseminating implementation experiences, and providing evidence about how value capture policies work on the ground are essential to overcome the disjunction between rhetoric and practice and to change the behavior and attitudes of public officials, landowners, and the community at large. A number of practical considerations and procedures can lead to more successful results.

- Assist public officials and decision makers in understanding that existing legal frameworks often are less restrictive than may be assumed.
- Relate value capture to fundamental principles of economic theory and good practices in public finance.
- Document how value capture has fostered investments in urban infrastructure and services and improved land use development.
- Shift the debate on value capture from ideological and social justice rhetoric to a more technical and practical context, grounded in evidence that it not only can be done, but has been done.

Promote Greater Public Understanding and Participation

Land value increments are captured more successfully from landowners and other stakeholders who perceive they are receiving greater benefits from a public intervention than those accruing from business as usual. Furthermore, value capture tools are more likely to succeed when used to solve a locally recognized problem. These steps can help to increase the chances of acceptance and success.

- Document and publicize successful demonstration projects, especially in countries where similar initiatives have been implemented, and explain the implications of increased social costs and lost opportunities when the potential value is not captured.
- Acknowledge that value capture is not simply a potential new revenue source but a tool to mitigate urban land market imperfections and facilitate urban planning and development.
- Illustrate how value capture has fostered investments in urban infrastructure and services and improved both local projects and large-scale developments.
- Emphasize that value capture policies can reduce speculation and corruption practices because land transactions are made more transparent and land value increments are less volatile.

REFERENCES

Afonso, José Roberto R., Erika Amorim Araujo, and Marcos Antonio Rios da Nóbrega. 2010. O imposto predial e territorial urbano (IPTU) no Brasil. Working Paper. Cambridge, MA: Lincoln Institute of Land Policy.

Almandoz, Arturo. 2004. The garden city in early twentieth-century in Latin America. *Urban History* 31(3): 437–452.

Alterman, Rachelle. 1989. *Evaluating linkage and beyond. The new method study for supply of affordable housing and its impact.* Cambridge, MA: Lincoln Institute of Land Policy.

Alterman, Rachelle. 2012. Land use regulations and property values: The "windfalls capture" idea revisited. In *Handbook of urban economics and planning*, eds. Nancy Brooks, Kieran Donaghy, and Gerrit-Jan Knaap. New York, NY: Oxford University Press.

Alvarez, Raul Daniel. 2009. Contribución de mejoras en Argentina. Casos de Rosario, Córdoba y Santa Fe. Presented at Primer Congreso Latinoamericano de Valorización, Bogotá, Colombia (March 11–12).

Angel, Shlomo, and Stephen K. Mayo. 1996. Enabling policies and their effects on housing sector performance: A global comparison. Presented at the Habitat II Conference, Istanbul, Turkey (June).

Barcia, Jakeline Jaramillo, and Wladimir Roser Ortiz.1996. Mercado del suelo en Quito. Municipio del Distrito Metropolitano de Quito, Dirección General de Planificación, #13. Quito, Ecuador.

Blackburn, Stephanie J., and David E. Dowall. 1991. *The tools for financing infrastructure.* Berkeley, CA: University of California Press.

Borrero Ochoa, Oscar. 2007. The effects of land policy on urban land prices in Bogotá. Working Paper. Cambridge, MA: Lincoln Institute of Land Policy.

Borrero Ochoa, Oscar. 2011. Betterment levy in Colombia: Relevance, procedures, and social acceptability. *Land Lines* 23(2): 14–19.

Borrero Ochoa, Oscar, Esperanza Durán, Jorge Hernández, and Magda Montaña. 2011. Evaluating the practice of betterment levies in Colombia: The experience of Bogotá and Manizales. Working Paper. Cambridge, MA: Lincoln Institute of Land Policy.

Bouillon, Cesar Patricio. 2012. *Room for development: Housing markets in Latin America and the Caribbean.* Hampshire, UK: Palgrave Macmillan Ltd. for Inter-American Development Bank.

Brain, Isabel, and Francisco Sabatini. 2006. Los precios del suelo en alza carcomen el subsidio habitacional, contribuyendo al deterioro en la calidad y localización de la vivienda social. *Revista ProUrbana* #4. Centro Políticas Publicas, Pontificia Universidad Católica de Chile.

Brito, Adriana Fausto, ed. 1998. *Suelo urbano y reservas territoriales: Politicas y mercado de suelo en América Latina.* Guadalajara, México: Universidad de Guadalajara and Lincoln Institute of Land Policy.

Brown, James H., and Martim O. Smolka. 1997. Capturing public value from public investments. In *land use and taxation: Applying the insights of Henry George*, ed. James H. Brown. Cambridge, MA: Lincoln Institute of Land Policy.

Burge, Gregory. 2010. The effects of development impact fees on local fiscal conditions. In *Municipal revenues and land policies*, eds. Gregory K. Ingram and Yu-Hung Hong. Cambridge, MA: Lincoln Institute of Land Policy.

Cáceres, Gonzalo, and Sabatini, Francisco. 2002. Recuperación de plusvalías: Reflexiones sobre su posible aplicación en las ciudades chilenas. *Revista Urbano* 5(6).

Chulipa Möller, Luiz Fernando. 2007. Contribución de mejoras: Un caso real en Brasil. In *Movilización social de la valorización de la tierra: Casos latinoamericano*, ed. María Clara Vejarano Alvarado. CD-ROM. Cambridge, MA: Lincoln Institute of Land Policy.

Cuenya, Beatriz, Silvia Pupareli, Gustavo Mosto, Haydé Cascella, Fernando Brunstein. Maria Di Loreto. 2003. *Relevamiento de métodos e instrumentos para la ponderación y recuperación de plusvalías urbanas generadas por la acción pública municipal.* Buenos Aires, Argentina: Consejo Nacional de Investigaciones Científicas y Técnicas (CONICET), Centro de Estudios Urbanos y Regionales (CEUR).

Cymbalista, Renato, and Paula Bittencourt Poggi Pollini. 2009. The implementation of the selling of building rights in Brazilian municipalities (2005–2006): Research based on the MUNIC–IBGE database. Unpublished report. Cambridge, MA: Lincoln Institute of Land Policy.

Cymbalista, Renato, and Paula Santoro. 2006. Outorga onerosa do direito de construir no Brasil: Entre a regulação e a arrecadação. Presented at Seminario e Curso de Política Fundiaria Municipal e Gestão Social da Valorização da Terra, São Paulo, Brazil (November).

Damasio, Claudia, ed. 2006. *Urbanizador social: Da informalidade à parceria.* Porto Alegre, Brasil: Livraria do Arquiteto and Lincoln Institute of Land Policy.

De Cesare, Claudia. 2012. *Improving the performance of the property tax in Latin America.* Policy Focus Report. Cambridge, MA: Lincoln Institute of Land Policy.

De Cesare, Claudia, Luiz Carlos P. da Silva Filho, Maurício Yoshinori Une, and Sheila Cristina Wend. 2003. Analyzing the feasibility of moving to a land value-based property tax system: A case study from Brazil. Working Paper. Cambridge, MA: Lincoln Institute of Land Policy.

Esteban, Ramón Alberto. 2007. Consorcio parque náutico San Fernando: Concesión de tierras municipales y recuperación de plusvalías. In *Movilización social de la valorización de la tierra: Casos latinoamericano*, ed. María Clara Vejarano Alvarado. CD-ROM. Cambridge, MA: Lincoln Institute of Land Policy.

Figueiredo, Vanessa G. B. 2005. Estratégias urbanas em busca do desenvolvimento local: o caso do projeto Eixo Tamanduathey em Santo André. Masters Thesis. São Paulo, Brazil: Faculdade de Arquitetura e Urbanismo, Universidade de São Paulo.

Fischel, William A. 2005. *The homevoter hypothesis: How home values influence local government taxation, school finance, and land-use policies.* Cambridge, MA: Harvard University Press.

Flores Dewey, Onesimo. 2011. The value of a promise: Housing price impacts of plans to build mass transit in Ecatepec, Mexico. Working Paper. Cambridge, MA: Lincoln Institute of Land Policy.

Furtado, Fernanda. 2000. Colombia. In *Land value taxation around the world,* third ed., Robert V. Andelson, 97–110. New York, NY: Wiley-Blackwell.

Furtado, Fernanda, and Claudia Acosta. 2013. Recuperación de plusvalías urbanas en Brasil, Colombia y otros países de América Latina: Legislación, instrumentos e implementación. Working Paper. Cambridge, MA: Lincoln Institute of Land Policy.

Furtado, Fernanda, Rosane Biassotto, and Camila Maleronka. 2012. *Outorga onerosa do direito de construer. Cadernos técnicos de regulamentação e implementaçãc.* Brasilia, Brasil: Ministério das Cidades do Brasil e Lincoln Institute of Land Policy.

Furtado, Fernanda, Vera F. Rezende, Teresa C. Oliveira, and Pedro Jorgensen Jr. 2010. Sale of building rights: Overview and evaluation of municipal experiences. Working Paper. Cambridge, MA: Lincoln Institute of Land Policy.

Furtado, Fernanda, and Gilberto Silva. 2010. Menos pode ser mais: Questoes acerca das relacoes entre o aproveitamento máximo e o aproveitamento ótimo dos terrenos urbanos. Presented at the 10th LARES International Conference, São Paulo, Brazil (September 15–17).

Gamarra Huayapa, Margarita. 2008. Experience with the betterment levy in Peru. Working Paper. Cambridge, MA: Lincoln Institute of Land Policy.

Garay, Alfredo. 2012. Puerto Madero: Balance de dos décadas de una intervención urbana. Unpublished Report. Cambridge, MA: Lincoln Institute of Land Policy.

García Bolivar, Luis Alberto. 2012. La contribución de valorización en la ciudad de Medellín. Paper presented at the Simposio técnicas y modelos sobre contribución de valorización: Experiencia nacional e internacional, Instituto de Estudios del Ministerio Público IEMP de la Procuraduría General de la Nación, en colaboración con el Instituto de Estudios Urbanos IEU de la Universidad Nacional de Colombia y el Lincoln Institute of Land Policy, Bogotá (April 17–18).

García Rojas, Elmer Fabio. 2012. Valorizacion por beneficio general: Aplicado en Santiago de Cali. Paper presented at the Simposio técnicas y modelos sobre contribución de valorización: Experiencia nacional e internacional, Instituto de Estudios del Ministerio Público IEMP de la Procuraduría General de la Nación, en colaboración con el Instituto de Estudios Urbanos IEU de la Universidad Nacional de Colombia y el Lincoln Institute of Land Policy, Bogotá (April 17–18).

Gazeta do Povo. 2012. Curitiba, Brazil: Edição XXX. December 13. *www.iba.com.br*

Gazeta do Povo. 2013. Curitiba, Brazil: Edição 30.412, February 23. *www.iba.com.br*

George, Henry. 1992. *Progress and poverty*. New York, NY: Schalkenbach Foundation.

Goelzer, Jorge, and Paulo Murad Saad. 1999. *Cost recovery performance of the benefit charge in the Paraná Urbano Program*. Curitiba, Brazil: PARANACIDADE.

Hagman, Donald G., and Dean J. Misczynski, eds. 1978. *Windfalls for wipeouts: Land value recapture and compensation*. Chicago, IL: American Society of Planning Officials.

Hong, Yu-Hung, and Isabel Brain. 2012. Land readjustment for urban development and post-disaster reconstruction. *Land Lines* 24(1): 2–9.

Hong, Yu-Hung, and Barrie Needham. 2007. *Analyzing land readjustment: Economics, law, and collective action*. Cambridge, MA: Lincoln Institute of Land Policy.

IBGE (Instituto Brasileiro de Geografia e Estatística). 2008. *Pesquisa de informações básicas municipais. Perfil dos municípios Brasileiros*. Rio de Janeiro, Brazil: IBGE. *http://www.ibge.gov.br*

Ingram, Gregory K., and Yu-Hung Hong, eds. 2012. *Value capture and land policies*. Cambridge, MA: Lincoln Institute of Land Policy.

Jaramillo González, Samuel. 1994. *Hacia una teória de la renta del suelo urbano*. Bogotá, Colombia: Ediciónes Uniandes.

Jaramillo González, Samuel. 1998. Consideraciones teóricas sobre la participación de los municipios en las plusvalías urbanas. *Desarrollo Urbano en Cifras* 4:164–176.

Jiménez Huerta, Edith R. 2013. Conformación de reservas territoriales en Aguascalientes como eje central para prevenir la informalidad. Presented at the Foro Latinoamericano sobre Instrumentos Notables de Intervención Urbana, Quito, Ecuador: Banco del Estado (Ecuador), Lincoln Institute of Land Policy, and Ministerio de las Ciudades de Brasil (May 6–10).

Kehew, Robert. 2002. Use of betterment fees in San Pedro Sula, Honduras. Unpublished Case Study. Cambridge, MA: Lincoln Institute of Land Policy.

Lawhon, Larry L. 2003. Development impact fee use by local governments. *Municipal Year Book*. Washington, DC: International City Management Association.

López Padilla, Ismael, and Salvador Gómez Rocha. 2013. La base seulo del impuesto a la propiedad. Presented at the Foro Latinoamericano sobre Instrumentos Notables de Intervención Urbana. Quito, Ecuador: Banco del Estado (Ecuador), Lincoln Institute of Land Policy, and Ministerio de las Ciudades de Brasil (May 6–10).

Lungo, Mario, ed. 2004. *Grandes proyectos urbanos*. San Salvador, El Salvador: UCA Editores, Universidad Centroamericana "Jose Simeon Canas" and Lincoln Institute of Land Policy.

Lungo, Mario, and Francisco Oporto. 1998. La captación de plusvalías inmobiliarias en El Salvador. Unpublished Report. Cambridge, MA: Lincoln Institute of Land Policy.

Maciel, Vladimir F. 2009. Transport infrastructure investment: Assessing the short-run effects of São Paulo's Beltway (Rodoanel) on land prices. Working Paper. Cambridge, MA: Lincoln Institute of Land Policy.

Maldonado Copello, Maria Mercedes. 2008. La Ley 388 de 1997 en Colombia: Algunos puntos de tensión en el proceso de su implementación. *Arquitectura, Ciudad y Entorno*, Ano III, 7 (Junio). Barcelona, Spain.

Maldonado Copello, Maria Mercedes, and Martim O. Smolka. 2003. Using value capture to benefit the poor: The Usme project in Colombia. *Land Lines* 15(3): 15–17.

Maleronka, Camila, and Fernanda Furtado. 2013. El otorgamiento oneroso del derecho de construir (OODC): La experiencia de São Paulo en la gestión pública de edificabilidades. Presented at the Foro Latinoamericano sobre Instrumentos Notables de Intervención Urbana, Quito, Ecuador: Banco del Estado (Ecuador), Lincoln Institute of Land Policy, and Ministerio de las Ciudades de Brasil (May 6–10).

Manon, Jorge, and José Merino Macon. 1977. *Financing urban and rural development through betterment levies: The Latin America experience*. Westport, CT: Praeger Publishers, Inc.

Maricato, E., and J. S. W. Ferreira. 2002. Operação urbana consorciada. In *Estatuto da cidade e reforma urbana: Novas perspectivas para as cidades brasileiras*, ed. L. N. Osório. Porto Alegre/São Paulo, Brasil: S.A. Fabris Editor.

Mendieta-López, J. C., and J. A. Perdomo-Calvo. 2007. Especificación y estimación de un modelo de precios hedónico espacial para evaluar el impacto de TransMilenio sobre el valor de la propiedad en Bogotá. Bogotá, Colombia: CEDE.

Mendive, Carlos. 2013. Presentación del caso Uruguayo. Presented at the Discussion Session on Using Land Value Capture Mechanisms for Financing Urban Development in Latin America and the Caribbean, Washington, DC (January 29–30).

Monserrat Guzman, Nilza. 2010. Contribución especial por plusvalía: Innovación en la gestión urbana municipal. México: Instituto Hacendario del Estado de México. *Foro Hacendario* 11(42): 23–26.

Montandon, Daniel T., and Felipe F. de Souza. 2007. *Land readjustment e operações consorciadas.* São Paulo: Romano Guerra Editora.

Municipalidad de Guatemala. 2013. *Evaluaciones de Impacto Vial.* Departamento de Planificación y Diseño.

Muñoz Gielen, Demetrio. 2010. *Capturing value increase in urban redevelopment: A study of how the economic value increase in urban redevelopment can be used to finance the necessary public infrastructure and other facilities.* Lieden, The Netherlands: Sidestone Press.

Muñoz-Raskin, R. 2006. Walking accessibility to bus rapid transit in Latin America: Does it affect property values? The case of Bogotá, Colombia. *TRB 86th Annual Meeting Compendium of Papers.* CD-ROM.

Oates, Wallace E., and Robert M. Schwab. 2009. The simple analytics of land value taxation. In *Land value taxation: Theory, evidence, and practice,* eds. Richard F. Dye and Richard W. England, 57–72. Cambridge, MA: Lincoln Institute of Land Policy.

Parodi, Gina. 2010. From debate to implementation: Colombia's territorial development law. Lecture. Cambridge, MA: Lincoln Institute of Land Policy.

Perdomo-Calvo, Jorge A., Camilo A. Mendoza-Álvarez, Juan Carlos Mendieta-López, and Andrés Francisco Baquero-Ruiz. 2007. Study of the effect of the TransMilenio mass transit project on the value of properties in Bogotá, Colombia. Working Paper. Cambridge, MA: Lincoln Institute of Land Policy.

Pereira, Gislene. 2012. Recuperação de mais valias urbanas por meio de contriuição de melhoria. O caso do Paraná, Brasil entre os anos 2000 e 2010. Unpublished Report, Cambridge, MA: Lincoln Institute of Land Policy.

Pérez Torres, Daniel E., and Rocio Cristina Acosta Peña. 2012. Evaluación de experiencias en la aplicación de contribuciones de mejoras e impuestos a la plusvalía en México. Unpublished Report. Cambridge, MA: Lincoln Institute of Land Policy.

Perló Cohen, Manuel, and Luis R. Zamorano Ruiz. 1999. Reform of the real estate tax system in Mexicali: 1989–1998. Working Paper. Cambridge, MA: Lincoln Institute of Land Policy.

Perló Cohen, Manuel, and Luis R. Zamorano Ruiz. 2001. Se justifica la aplicación del impuesto a la plusvalía en México? In *Recuperación de plusvalías en América Latina: Alternativas para el desarrollo urbano,* eds. Martim Smolka y Fernando Furtado. Santiago, Chile: EureLibros. Pontificia Universidad Católica de Chile and Lincoln Institute of Land Policy.

Peterson, George E. 2009. *Unlocking land values to finance urban infrastructure.* Washington, DC: World Bank and Public-Private Infrastructure Advisory Facility (PPIAF).

Petrobras. 2013. *http://www.comperj.com.br/Apresentacao.aspx*

Pinilla, Juan Felipe Pineda. 2013. Anuncio de proyecto y avalúos de referencia como mecanismo de control a los precios del suelo: Estudio de caso Operación Estratégica Nuevo Usme, Bogotá, Colombia. Presented at the Foro Latinoamericano sobre Instrumentos Notables de Intervención Urbana. Quito, Ecuador: Banco del Estado (Ecuador), Lincoln Institute of Land Policy, and Ministerio de las Ciudades de Brasil (May 6–10).

Pinilla, Juan Felipe Pineda, and Alejandro Florián. 2011. Experiencia e innovación en cultura tributaria la campaña del 110% con Bogotá. Unpublished Report. Cambridge, MA: Lincoln Institute of Land Policy.

Rabello de Castro, Sonia. 2006. O conceito de justa indenização nas expropriações imobiliárias urbanas: Justiça social ou enriquecimento sem causa? Rio de Janeiro, Brazil: *Revista Forens* 388: 221–245.

Rabello de Castro, Sonia. 2012. Faculty profile. *Land Lines* 24(1): 18–19.

Reyes, Fernando. 1980. El sistema de valorizacion y sus implicaciones economicas. Thesis. Bogotá, Colombia: Universidad de Bogotá Jorge Tadeo Lozano.

Rezende, Vera F. 1982. *Planejamento urbano e ideologia: Quatro planos para a cidade do Rio de Janeiro.* Brazil: Editora Civilização Brasileira, Grupo Editorial Record.

Rezende, Vera F. 2005. O jogo de verde com branco: Lúcio Costa em defesa do Plano Piloto da Barra da Tijuca e Baixada de Jacarepaguá. Presented at the 6th Seminario Docomomo. *Conference Proceedings,* Niteroi, Brazil: EdUFF Editora da Universidade Federal Fluminense.

Rodríguez, D. A., and F. Targa. 2004. Value of accessibility to Bogotá's bus rapid transit system. *Transport Reviews* 24 (5): 587–610.

Rodríguez, Daniel A., and Carlos H. Mojica. 2008. Land value impacts of bus rapid transit: The case of Bogotá's TransMilenio. *Land Lines* 20(2).

Rodríguez, Vanessa, and Diego Aulestia. 2013. Incentivos por el cobro de Contribución Especial de Mejoras para el financiamiento de la infraestructura pública. Presented at the Foro Latinoamericano sobre Instrumentos Notables de Intervención Urbana. Quito, Ecuador: Banco del Estado (Ecuador), Lincoln Institute of Land Policy, and Ministerio de las Ciudades de Brasil (May 6–10).

Rojas Eberhard, María Cristina, and Beatriz Elena Rave. 2013. Reajuste de tierras en Medellín, Colombia. Presented at the Foro Latinoamericano sobre Instrumentos Notables de Intervención Urbana. Quito, Ecuador: Banco del Estado (Ecuador), Lincoln Institute of Land Policy, and Ministerio de las Ciudades de Brasil (May 6–10).

Salandía, Luis Fernando Valverde. 2012. Desafios metropolitanos à gestão pública de apropriação do espaço urbano no leste metropolitano do Rio de Janeiro. Universidade Federal Fluminense, Niterói: *Tese (Doutorado em Geografia).*

Sandroni, Paulo. 2001. Plusvalías urbanas en Brasil: Creación, recuperación y apropiación en la ciudad de São Paulo. In *Recuperación de plusvalías en América Latina,* eds. Martim Smolka y Fernanda Furtado. Santiago, Chile: EureLibros. Pontificia Universidad Católica de Chile y Lincoln Institute of Land Policy.

Sandroni, Paulo Henrique. 2010. A new financial instrument of value capture in São Paulo: Certificates of additional construction. In *Municipal revenues and land policies*, eds. Gregory K. Ingram and Yu-Hung Hong, 218–240. Cambridge, MA: Lincoln Institute of Land Policy.

Sandroni, Paulo Henrique. 2011. Urban value capture in São Paulo using a two-part approach: Created land (solo criado) and sale of building rights (outorga onerosa do direito de construir): An analysis of the impact of the basic coefficient of land use as a tool of the 2002 Master Plan. Working Paper. Cambridge, MA: Lincoln Institute of Land Policy.

Sandroni, Paulo, ed. 2012. *Dicionario de economia do seculo XXI, 7a edição.* Rio de Janeiro, Brasil: Record.

Sandroni, Paulo Henrique. 2013. Certificados de potencial adicional de construcción (CEPAC) en la financiación de grandes proyectos de desarrollo urbano: El caso de São Paulo. Presented at the Foro Latinoamericano sobre Instrumentos Notables de Intervención Urbana. Quito, Ecuador: Banco del Estado (Ecuador), Lincoln Institute of Land Policy, and Ministerio de las Ciudades de Brasil (May 6–10).

Serra, M. V., David E. Dowall, Diana Meirelles da Motta, and Michael Donovan. 2005. Urban land markets and urban land development: An examination of three Brazilian cities: Brasilia, Curitiba, and Recife. In *Estudos estratéicos de apoio às politicas urbanas para os grupos de baixa renda no Brasil (Enabling strategy for moving upgrading to scale in Brazil*, eds. M. V. Serra and D. M. da Motta. CD-ROM. Washington, DC: Cities Alliance.

Shoup, Donald. 1994. Is underinvestment in public infrastructure an anomaly? In *Methodology for land and housing market analysis*, eds. Gareth Jones and Peter M. Ward. Cambridge, MA: Lincoln Institute of Land Policy with London: UCL Press.

Sietchiping, Remy, ed. 2011. *Innovative land and property taxation.* Nairobi, Kenya: UN-Habitat, Global Land Tool Network.

Smolka, Martim O. 1994. Bridging conceptual and methodological issues in the study of second-hand property markets the city of Rio de Janeiro. In *Methodology for land and housing market analysis*, eds. Gareth Jones and Peter M. Ward, 179–196. Cambridge, MA: Lincoln Institute of Land Policy with London: UCL Press.

Smolka, Martim O. 2011. Precios elevados (e inaccesibles) de la tierra urbana habilitada. In *Periubanizacion y sustentabilidad en grandes ciudades*, eds. A. G. Aguilar e Irma Escamilla. México: Instituto de Geografia-UNAM.

Smolka, Martim O. 2012. A new look at value capture in Latin America. *Land Lines* 24(3): 10–15.

Smolka, Martim O., and David Amborski. 2007. Value capture for urban development: An inter-American comparison. Working Paper. Cambridge, USA: Lincoln Institute of Land Policy.

Smolka, Martim O., and Claudia P. Damasio. 2005. The social urbanizer: Porto Alegre's land policy experiment. *Land Lines* 17(2): 11–14.

Smolka, Martim O., and Fernanda Furtado. 2001. *Recuperación de plusvalías en América Latina: Alternativas para el desarrollo urbano.* Santiago, Chile: EureLibros. Pontificia Universidad Católica de Chile and Lincoln Institute of Land Policy.

Smolka, Martim O., and A. X. Iracheta Cenecorta. 1999. Mobilizing land value increments to provide serviced land for the poor. *Land Lines* 11(4).

Soffiatti, Rubens Valério Franco. 2012. A contribuição de melhoria como instrumento de recuperação da Mais-Valia Fundiária Urbana: Estudo de caso Eixo Urbano "Linha Verde." Masters Thesis. Curitiba, Paraná, Brasil: Pontificia Universidade Católica Do Paraná, Escola de Arquitetura e Design, Programa de Pós-Graduação em Gestão Urbana.

Teixeira, Maria Fernanda and Tomas Moreira. 2011. Solo criado: Uma analise do processo de aplicação do instrumentos em Curitiba. Rio de Janeiro, Brasil: *Anais do Encontro Nacional da Associação Nacional de Planejamento Urbanos— ANPUR.* CD-ROM.

UN-Habitat. 1976. The Vancouver Declaration. United Nations Conference on Human Settlements, Vancouver, Canada (May 31–June 11). *http://habitat.igc.org/vancouver/van-decl.htm*

UN-Habitat. 2008. *State of the world's cities 2008/2009 – Harmonious cities.* London, UK and Sterling, USA: Earthscan for the United Nations Human Settlements Programme.

Uzon, Néia. 2007. Uso de la transferencia del potencial constructivo para la adquisición de inmuebles: la experiencia de Porto Alegre. In *Movilización social de la valorización de la tierra: Casos latinoamericano*, ed. María Clara Vejarano Alvarado. CD-ROM. Cambridge, MA: Lincoln Institute of Land Policy.

Vainer, Carlos. 2000. Os liberais tambem fazem planejamento urbano? In *Cidade do Pensamento Unico: Demanchando Consensos*, eds. O. Arantes, C. Vainer, e E. Maricato, 75–104. Rio de Janeiro, Brasil: Editora Vozes.

Verajano Alvarado, María Clara, ed. 2007. *Movilización social de la valorización de la tierra: Casos latinoamerican.* CD-ROM. Cambridge, MA: Lincoln Institute of Land Policy.

Vetter, D. M., R. M. Massena, and E. F. Rodrígues. 1979. Espaço, valor da terra e equidade dos investimentos em infraestrutura do município do Rio de Janeiro. *Revista Brasileira de Geografia* 41(1-2): 32–71.

Vetter, D. M., R. M. Massena, and M. F. Vetter. 2011. Land values and the affordability of lower income housing: Three municipalities in the Rio de Janeiro metropolitan region. Internal Report. Rio de Janeiro, Brazil: Land Markets in Latin American and Caribbean Cities project of the Latin American and Caribbean Research Network, Inter-American Development Bank, by David Vetter Consultoria Econômica Ltda.

Vickrey, William. 1999. Simplifications, progression, and a level playing field. In *Land value taxation: The equitable and efficient source of public finance*, ed. Kenneth Wenzer, 17–23. Armonk, NY: M.E. Sharpe.

Villamil, Ivan Domínquez. 2000. An analysis of the use of valorization in Bogotá. Master of Regional Planning Thesis. Ithaca, NY: Cornell University.

Walker, Kevin Alan Sherper. 2000. In search of the progressive city: An examination of the special assessment in Bogotá, Colombia. Master of Regional Planning Thesis. Ithaca, NY: Cornell University.

Walters, Lawrence C. 2012. *Land value capture in policy and practice.* Salt Lake City, Utah. Romney Institute, Brigham Young University.

Whitaker Ferreira, Joao Sette. 2012. Linha Verde na bolsa e operação de Alto Risco. *Gazeta do Povo*, June 7.

Xavier, Helia Nacif. 2011. Tensoes entre planejamento urbano e ação imediata: A operação interligada na cidade do Rio de Janeiro (1997–2000). Doctoral Thesis. Rio de Janeiro, Brazil: Universidade Federal do Rio de Janeiro.

ACKNOWLEDGMENTS

Special thanks to the following Lincoln Institute of Land Policy staff for very helpful comments on earlier versions: Gregory K. Ingram, president and CEO; Joan Youngman, senior fellow and chair of the Department of Valuation and Taxation; and Anna Sant'Anna, senior research associate in the Program on Latin America and the Caribbean. Particular appreciation is given to Ann LeRoyer, former senior editor and director of publications, for her editing work and for managing the design and production of this report.

In addition, gratitude to David Vetter of Vetter Consultoría Económica Ltda., based in Rio de Janeiro, Brazil, for his insightful review of the full draft; and to Fernanda Furtado, professor and researcher in the School of Architecture and Urbanism at the Fluminense Federal University, Niterói, State of Rio de Janeiro, Brazil, for suggestions when the project was in its early stages.

This report also benefitted from numerous insights and specific inputs from experts throughout Latin America who are directly involved with the implementation of value capture tools. Deep appreciation is extended to all those listed below who provided timely updates on local issues and practices; critical clarifications of how value capture instruments operate and their impacts in different jurisdictions; and many of the graphic illustrations and photographs. The author, however, is fully responsible for any remaining misinterpretations, errors, and omissions.

Claudio Acioly Jr., head, Capacity Development Unit, UN-HABITAT, Nairobi, Kenya

Hernando Arenas, geographer and urban planner, Institute of Urban Development, Bogotá, Colombia

Zulma Bolivar, architect and planner; president of the Urbanism Metropolitan Institute (IMUTC), Caracas, Venezuela

Oscar Armando Borrero Ochoa, economist and professor, National University of Colombia, Bogotá; and private consultant, Borrero Ochoa & Asociados, Bogotá, Colombia

Gonzalo Cáceres, professor, Institute of Urban and Territorial Studies, Catholic University of Chile, Santiago

Rosemary Campans, architect-urbanist, Municipal Urbanism Institute, Rio de Janeiro, Brazil

Rosario Casanova, engineer, University of the Republic, Montevideo, Uruguay

Luiz Fernando Chulipa Möller, consultant in property assessment and taxation, Porto Alegre, Brazil

Beatriz Cuenya, director, Centre of Urban and Regional Studies, National Scientific and Technical Research Council (CEUR-CONICET), Buenos Aires, Argentina

Roberto Eibenshultz, professor and researcher, National Metropolitan Autonomous University of Mexico (UNAM), Mexico DF, Mexico

Diego Erba, fellow, Program on Latin America and the Caribbean, Lincoln Institute of Land Policy

Ramon Esteban, city councilor; former secretary of planning, Municipality of San Fernando, Province of Buenos Aires, Argentina

Alfredo Garay, professor, School of Architecture, Design, and Urban Planning, University of Buenos Aires, Argentina

Silvia García Vettorazzi, architect and vice-director, Urbanística Public Space Worshop, Guatemala City, Guatemala

Cynthia Goytia, economist, professor and director, Masters in Urban Economics, Torcuato Di Tella University, Buenos Aires, Argentina

Alfonso Iracheta Cenecorta, coordinator, Program on Urban and Environmental Studies, Colegio Mexiquense, Toluca, Mexico

Ignacio Carlos Kunz Bolaños, researcher, National Autonomous University of Mexico (UNAM), Consultant, Querétaro, Mexico

André Kwak, urban studies manager, São Paulo Urbanismo, Municipality of São Paulo, Brazil

Heliana Lombardi Artigiani, architect and assessor, Secretariat of Urban Development, Municipality of São Paulo, Brazil

Maria Mercedes Maldonado, professor, National University of Colombia; and Secretary of Housing, Bogotá, Colombia

Camila Maleronka, architect, public administrator, São Paulo Urbanismo, São Paulo, Brazil

Allan Mazariegos, architect, Department of Public Works, Municipality of Guatemala City, Guatemala

Iris Elizabeth Medina Torres, specialist in planning, Municipality of Lima, Peru

Carlos Mendive, economist, University of the Republic, Montevideo, Uruguay

Catalina Molinatti, independent consultant for several Argentinean local governments; formerly developed land value capture instruments, Municipality of Córdoba, Argentina

Carlos Morales Schechinger, senior expert on urban land management and policies, Institute for Housing and Urban Development Studies (IHS), Erasmus University, Rotterdam, The Netherlands

Angel Ricardo Núñez Fernández, United Nations Development Program, Havana, Cuba

Gislene Pereira, professor and director, Laboratory of Housing and Urban Development, Federal University of Paraná, Brazil

Juan Felipe Pinilla, independent consultant and researcher on land policy, property, and urban law issues, Bogotá, Colombia

Eglaisa M. Pontes Cunha, educator and capacity building manager, Ministry of the Cities, Brasilia, Brazil

Sonia Rabello de Castro, professor and researcher, Law School of the State University of Rio de Janeiro, Brazil

Eduardo Ramírez Favela, former president, CABIN (Commission for the Assessment of National Assets), in association with the Santa Fe project, Mexico DF, Mexico

Beatriz Rave, architect and general manager, Housing Authority for Antioquia Province, (Empresa de Vivienda de Antioquia VIVA), Medellín, Colombia

Eduardo Reese, professor of urban management and planning, Conurbano Institute, General Sarmiento National University, Buenos Aires, Argentina

Vera Rezende, professor and researcher on urban planning, School of Architecture and Urbanism, Fluminense Federal University, Niterói, State of Rio de Janeiro, Brazil

Daniel Rodríguez, director, Carolina Transportation Program; and associate professor, Department of City and Regional Planning, University of North Carolina at Chapel Hill

Vanessa Rodríguez, independent consultant, Quito, Ecuador

María Cristina Rojas Eberhard, independent consultant for various Colombian public institutions, Bogotá

Paulo Sandroni, private consultant; professor, Getulio Vargas Foundation, São Paulo, Brazil

Martha Siniacoff, director of cadastre and assessments, Municipality of Montevideo, Uruguay

Nadia Somekh, director, Department of Historic Heritage; president, Municipal Council of Historic, Cultural and Environmental Heritage, Municipality of São Paulo, Brazil

Alvaro Uribe, architect, planner, and professor, University of Panama; member of the advisory council, Panama Ministry of Housing

Néia Uzon, independent consultant, Porto Alegre, Brazil

Luis Fernando Valverde Salandia, architect, Secretariat for Housing, Municipality of Rio de Janeiro, Brazil

Maria Clara Vejarano, professor and researcher, National University of Colombia, Bogotá; and doctoral candidate, Federal University of Rio de Janeiro, Brazil

Stella Zuccolini, architect and planner, Housing and Urban Planning Ministry, Montevideo, Uruguay